By Betty and Jock Leslie-Melville

Raising Daisy Rothschild
Elephant Have the Right of Way
There's a Rhino in the Rosebed, Mother

By Betty Leslie-Melville

That Nairobi Affair

Raising Daisy Rothschild

BETTY and JOCK
LESLIE-MELVILLE

Simon and Schuster
New York

Published by Simon and Schuster
A Division of Gulf & Western Corporation
Simon & Schuster Building
Rockefeller Center
1230 Avenue of the Americas
New York, New York 10020

Designed by Elizabeth Woll
Manufactured in the United States of America

1   2   3   4   5   6   7   8   9   10

Library of Congress Cataloging in Publication Data

Leslie-Melville, Betty.
Raising Daisy Rothschild.

1.   Giraffes—Legends and stories.   I.   Leslie-
Melville, Jock, joint author.   II.   Title.
QL795.G55L47   599'.7357   77-22580
ISBN 0-671-22865-X

For all wild animals everywhere who can neither speak out, nor vote, for their own cause—which is survival.

Contents

11

Introduction

by LADY HUXLEY

Sitting here in my home in Hampstead I am indeed a long way from Africa, but Betty and Jock Leslie-Melville's vivid, fascinating and lively story is like a magic carpet; it flies me right back to that indestructible love affair which started in 1929 when I first lost my heart to Africa—and to giraffe. Moreover, Betty and Jock's tale of their own love affair with their giraffe Daisy Rothschild vividly reminds me of my encounter last November: Daisy was licking Betty's pretty face with that seventeen-inch purple elastic tongue and purloining a carrot from Betty's lips. It was a most improbable sight. But then, so is a giraffe.

Darwin, in the throes and perplexities of giving birth to evolution, confessed that "the sight of a feather in a peacock's tail made me sick whenever I gazed at it." He does not, unfortunately, record what he felt when he looked at a giraffe, except to characterize its

13

tail as an excellent fly disperser. But was there, in cold fact, any simple justification, any more than there was for the fabulous jewel in the peacock's feather, for that singular creation, that extravagance of angles, that triangular elongation coated with crazy paving, the modern and somewhat modest descendant of a long experiment in giraffedom?

True, the "niche" of high grazing had been left open for a long-necked animal that could eat a dish of thorns off the top of trees: the neck vertebrae stretched out their bony cells to the utmost, even while remaining the regimental seven of the Class of Mammals. Likewise its front legs, elongated up to their shoulders, made terms with shorter hind legs by a diagonal backbone. Yet I defy any surrealist artist to *invent* a giraffe.

But we are not here concerned with its preposterous appearance; we are concerned, far more importantly, with the bond that Betty and Jock created—not without serious risks to themselves and their property—with Daisy and, later, younger Marlon: giraffe doomed to be destroyed by human encroachment into their wilderness. The larger part of that unusual adoption—on both sides—was love (Lorenz calls it "imprinting" on the animal side); curious as it may sound, love is essential in any so-called taming of wild animals. The rest—bed and breakfast, security and patient watchfulness—is almost incidental.

> Love begets love, then never be
> Unsoft to him who's smooth to thee.
> Tigers and bears, I've heard say
> For proffered love will love repay. . . .
>
> Herrick

In most cases, the taming of wild animals is not a painless or gratuitous gesture. You invite a giraffe to share your garden, and there won't be much garden left. I saw Daisy and Marlon delicately nibble off all the bougainvillea flowers from the facade of the house, as well as green shoots of acacia, wild gardenia, and many other growing things. The house itself was supposedly out of bounds to giraffe, but the long neck could carry an inquisitive velvet mouth through the windows right into the conservatory where some succulent house plants were thriving. At Betty's gentle reproach, the lambent eyes with their film-star eyelashes looked pained and misunderstood. One could prophesy—unless strong measures were taken—

14

the bright sofa covers and curtains sacrificed to a playful nibble and a nonchalant toss of the head.

But Jock and Betty's story is more than just about giraffe; it brings out the conflict between the wildlife that once dominated the vast continent and the human population which is now threatening its very survival. Daisy and Marlon Rothschild are adopted because there are just about 180 Rothschild giraffe left, and they are doomed to swift extinction when the land on which they live is turned into African smallholdings. The problem, and the population explosion, have been before us for over half a century, and one of its first exponents was my late husband, Julian Huxley.

Jock and Betty have taken the gallant and practical action of doing their bit to help. In that, as well as in the story of their confrontation with rarely tamed animals, they have enlarged our knowledge of the complexities and complicities of the survival of life, its terrible vulnerability, and our own grave responsibility. They have done it with their own sense of fun and their charm, enhancing that of Daisy and Marlon, and though the matter is serious, it bears lightly upon the reader. The best of luck to the outcome!

1

A Thanksgiving
Twiga

As he put the third stitch in my hand the doctor in the emergency ward of Nairobi Hospital said, "This is the first time I've ever had to write under Cause of Injury, 'Due to giraffe sucking patient's thumb.' "

"She didn't mean to hurt me," I said apologetically.

"A baby giraffe thrusts—like a calf—when it suckles," explained Jock, my husband, who was standing next to us watching the needle go in and out, "but Betty didn't know that."

"Where would I ever have seen calves thrusting? In Baltimore? In Central Park? Doctor, do you think I'll get G.D.?"

"G.D.?" the doctor repeated.

"Giraffe disease."

"You'll have to have a tetanus shot," he smiled. "Tell me, does this giraffe of yours—Daisy, you call her?—always suck your thumb?"

"Sometimes mine and sometimes Jock's. She thinks Jock is her mother. He does look more like a giraffe than I do, don't you think? They say people grow to look like their pets, and I certainly am beginning to *feel* like a giraffe—I wonder if my neck is getting any longer—but Jock already looked like one."

The doctor glanced at Jock uneasily.

I guess living with a giraffe does take a while to get used to, but we've reached the stage where it doesn't even seem odd that our giraffe looks in the window at us to see if we're talking on the telephone, nor that we may put our hand over the receiver and whisper loudly to her, "I'll be out in a minute, Daisy."

The reason for covering the receiver is that one time a friend asked, "Who are you talking to?" (No one we know ever says, "To whom are you talking?") to which I replied, "Daisy."

"Daisy who?"

"Daisy Rothschild, my giraffe."

"It's time for your injection, Betty."

It *is* hard to say how we got ourselves into this. Looking back, I think it was all Doria Block's fault. One day when she came for lunch she was gazing out across our lawn watching Tom, Dick, and Harry, the three wild giraffe who live on our property most of the time, and said, "Why don't you get a baby? One of the Craigs'?"

"I have no idea what you're talking about," I told her.

"David and Delia Craig are selling their ranch at Soy, and it's filled with Rothschild giraffe—the only Rothschild left in Kenya, as a matter of fact. They'll all be poached within a year and I know they'd be delighted if you would save one."

Neither Jock nor I is what you might call an "animal lover." We find that many people in the States take it for granted that we are wildlife experts simply because we live in Africa. We are more absorbed with the political developments here than with wildlife, and every time someone asks us what our favorite species of animal is we answer, "Man." We have resisted having any living creatures for which we are responsible, except Shirley Brown, our Labrador, and Jock says the three children can also stay, but that's it.

However, that night Jock and I got talking about how much we did enjoy having Tom, Dick, and Harry around. We had moved into our house about a year earlier and were delighted to find that the three old bull giraffe also considered our land home. The house stands on three hundred acres in Langata, a suburb of Nairobi, a mile from Nairobi Game Park. We could afford to buy only fifteen acres, but the rest of the land has not been sold yet, so in effect the three hundred acres are ours. Mount Kilimanjaro looms in view 110 miles away; perhaps the giraffe like the view as much as we do. Whatever the reason, they live here, too. It is a thrilling sight to sit in the living room watching the tallest animals in the world standing in front of the tallest mountain in Africa. Or they may stroll down the driveway, munching the trees they fancy, destroying our shrubs and stomping the flowers along the way. Sometimes they just stand there for an hour or so watching us or the gardener work, and they sleep on the front lawn almost every night.

Giraffe are *enormous*. I don't think most people realize how gigantic they are. I knew they were the tallest animals in the world, but eighteen feet is *really* tall and three thousand pounds is *really* huge, and until you appreciate that Jock, who is six feet three inches, could (if he wanted to commit suicide) walk right underneath one without stooping down, you won't grasp what giants they really are. Up close they seem like dinosaurs.

So we named our three Tom, Dick, and Harry, and their three friends who visit them regularly about once a week Larry, Moe, and Curley. How can we tell them apart? The same way you can tell your white poodles apart. Big Dick is easy because he's the largest, over eighteen feet tall, Tom has a very long slim white face, and Harry is much darker. Anyway, they are aging and won't live beyond thirty years old, and that night Jock and I were discussing how sad it would be when they keeled over, thereby depriving us of the enchantment of their presence.

"If we got a baby Rothschild giraffe," I said cautiously, "we'd be sure to have one around for the next twenty-five or thirty years. It wouldn't be much trouble—it would live outside and just eat the trees and we wouldn't have to *do* anything for it." Ha—little did I know of what I spoke.

When we called Doria for the Craigs' number she had had second thoughts. "Why get involved with something you don't know anything about?" she asked.

But we had already decided to once again get involved with something we didn't know anything about, and the Craigs said yes, they would be delighted if we would take one of their young giraffe. After all, we'd be helping to save a species—there were only 180 of the Rothschild left in Kenya.

How do we get one? we asked.

Well, they don't respond too well to tranquilizer drugs, they told us, especially the babies. Evidently there is something in the animal tranquilizers to which giraffe are allergic, and the fatalities are high. There is only one way, they said: we must get hold of Jock Rutherfurd and his horse.

Jock had gone to school with Rutherfurd but hadn't seen him in years. (As this story proceeds I will refer to him as Rutherfurd to avoid confusion with my Jock.) It turned out that nobody else had seen him for some time, either, but we left messages everywhere and with everyone, and after about six weeks, when we were on the point of giving up, he arrived one afternoon for tea. (For Rutherfurd tea always consists of a warm beer.) He is a blond forty-fivish former major with the Kenya Regiment with the longest eyelashes ever (next to giraffe) and has an elusive charm and an interesting way of wrinkling up his nose when he laughs—which is often.

He had managed the Craigs' farm for years and had seen what was going to happen—that the land would be divided into smallholdings and sold to Africans and all the giraffe would be killed. In anticipation of that dreaded event, he had experimented capturing some of them in order to move them to safer places. Yes, he had raised a few himself. They were delightful animals, he told us—friendly, gentle, fun. Suzannah was a favorite of his. She ate the soap out of his second-floor bathroom and he had to keep his polo stick next to the tub to knock her on the head when she put it in through the window. She also ate laundry off the line and ran up to his car for a kiss every night when he came home.

Beats Tom, Dick, or Harry, we thought. In fact, they seemed rather colorless next to her. "So," we asked, "how do we get one?"

"I'll get on my horse and rope one for you," he answered, making it sound like roundup time at the dude ranch. "Then we put it in a stable up there and give it a little milk for a few days. Then bring it here to Nairobi."

"How?" we asked, pedants that we are.

"Put it in that minibus that you have out front," he answered.

"Put a giraffe in a *minibus*? How do we keep it there for the 225-mile drive?"

"Sit on it," he answered, with his nose-wrinkling smile.

It seemed so easy. Boy, did we have a lot to learn. He didn't mention the fact that an African was killed by one of the giraffe at Soy. He didn't mention the fact that *his* chances of being killed about equaled his chances of staying alive. He didn't mention the fact that there is a very high mortality rate among captured babies, and that if they do survive they have to be fed for nearly two years. He didn't mention . . . Rutherfurd made it all sound easy, but it isn't. However, we didn't know that then, and in three weeks' time we found ourselves driving merrily to Soy for the big capture.

On the way we drove through bamboo forests, crossed the Equator in a cold mist at over nine thousand feet, and passed the Burnt Forest Police Station. Five hours after leaving home Jock, Rick (the older of our two sons), Shirley Brown, and I arrived at a local club, where we were to meet Rutherfurd.

He was having lunch but was disenchanted with the steak, so he gave it to Shirley Brown, who took it outside and buried it. That about sums up the food at the club. He had arranged for us to stay at the little cottage on the Lewa Downs Estate, which is the name of the Craigs' ranch. It came by that name through a somewhat more complicated story than Burnt Forest. Two hundred miles from Soy, at the northwest foot of Mount Kenya, there is a spring which provides the last little patch of green before the vast and arid Northern Province. Except for a few water holes where the Somali and Boran nomads water their camels, and a couple of rivers which cut through the hot flat territory, the place is dry and desolate. Two or three years ago an archaeologist who was a member of Richard Leakey's team digging for fossils there wandered away from the camp, got lost, and died of thirst in the desert. In the early days, safari parties heading for the oasis of Mount Marsabit in the middle of the desert would pause at the spring, where the Craigs' other farm is now situated, before beginning the long hot haul into the wilderness. On the return trip, usually weeks later, they were so pleased to see the cool water gushing from the ground that they would camp there for several days while they broke open cases of champagne, carried there for their sustenance by porters or ox wagons. The champagne would flow nearly as fast as the spring while the happy safariers unwound and drank themselves silly. The Africans, deadly accurate with their nicknames and descriptions, referred laughingly to the place as Lewa Springs. *Lewa* in Swahili means drunk. When Delia Craig's father acquired the spring and the land immediately around it, he was so amused by the name that he retained it and christened both his property there and the one at Soy Lewa Downs, combining the blunt Swahili word with the softer English description of gently rolling hills. The land they were selling, their eighteen thousand acres at Soy, lies a few miles from the western wall of the Great Rift Valley. Except for the occasional

21

fence and the presence of some beef cattle, the place remains unaltered by man and is simply a patch of wild Africa.

As we bumped our way to the cottage in an isolated corner of the ranch where we were to stay, Jock asked Rutherfurd, "Didn't Peter Hankin work for the Craigs?"

"Yes, he did," answered Rutherfurd.

"Is he still around?"

"No, he got eaten up by a lion," he replied cheerfully.

I had a small feeling right then that something was funny as far as Rutherfurd and understatements went, and the premonition was not erased by his saying as we alighted from the car to go into the cottage, "Watch out for pythons, there're a few about."

"Anything else?"

"The occasional leopard," he answered casually.

After dumping our luggage and supplies we piled back into the car and drove around Lewa Downs looking for giraffe. We found two large herds of about forty each. While watching the second through binoculars Rutherfurd said, "There's the one I'll go for."

I felt sad. Take that baby away from its mother? Its friends? Its home? But I had to face reality: any giraffe not removed from Soy would be poached by the new settlers and dead within a year. Even if the translocation of some of the Rothschild to a safe area was attempted, babies would get separated from mothers and would die. Also, I knew that if we succeeded in capturing it, and it lived, it would have a happy life among the other wild giraffe on our property in Langata.

Both Rutherfurd and the Craigs had told us that girl giraffe are less trouble than boys. They are not so likely to be adventuresome or to wander off (as is true of dogs) and have generally sweeter dispositions. We had set our heart on a girl, therefore, but Rutherfurd explained there was no way of telling the difference during the chase.

The next morning at eight when Rutherfurd arrived at the cottage he was friendly, as always, and casual, but there was an underlying tension showing just before the event as seen in racing drivers, steeplechase jockeys, and others of that ilk who voluntarily commit themselves to dangerous undertakings. He was wearing jeans and a shirt; he didn't even have a polo helmet, and wanted nothing but a glass of milk. Of medium height and weight, he is an excellent horseman, quiet, intelligent, a loner and a wild man—for he is possibly the only person in the world who will attempt the capture of a giraffe from a horse. He modestly denies this kind of description, giving credit instead to his horse Douglas. True, Douglas is as much of an individual as Rutherfurd and is the only *horse* in the world prepared to attempt this hazardous undertaking. It took Rutherfurd three years to train him to go in among a herd of giraffe.

Horses, along with other animals including predators, have a tremendous respect for giraffe because of the lethal kick with which the giraffe protect themselves. Mild and beautiful, they are never aggressive, but with a terrible forward punching kick of the front feet they will defend themselves even against lion. As if that were not bad enough, the land that the Rothschild herd lives on at Soy is also potentially lethal for horse and rider because it is pocked with ant-bear holes two feet wide and three feet deep which are hidden in the long grass. The nocturnal ant bear, or aardvark, dig these enormous holes with effortless ease in the matter of a few minutes while searching for termites, and whether they find what they are looking for or not, the hole remains for years afterwards, camouflaged by grass and scrub. I fell into three holes while walking across the terrain. In fact the land is so bad that once someone in a truck who was trying to follow Rutherfurd on his horse to watch a capture broke his leg—sitting in the truck!

However, Douglas doesn't seem to mind about such hazards. Between them he and Rutherfurd have developed a remarkable and probably the only workable relationship. Douglas concentrates solely on the ground. He does not look to see in which direction he is going and has no idea whether Rutherfurd will ride him into a tree or over a precipice. Rutherfurd, on the other hand, wastes no time worrying about what is going on underfoot, but concentrates exclusively on the maneuvering, and on extracting the power from Douglas at the right moment in order to get alongside a baby to rope it.

No one in his right mind would ride a horse over Lewa Downs, and no one but Rutherfurd will ride Douglas, who is said to be mad too.

The two other members of the suicide squad are Kiborr, an African *syce* (groom), and his horse Turbo (Jet), the only other horse in the world who will go near giraffe. Turbo does it not because he is mentally ill in the same way as Douglas, but because his particular deficiency in the brain department manifests itself through being madly in love with Douglas—going everywhere Douglas goes, doing whatever Douglas does—despite being blind in one eye. Kiborr rides this one-eyed gay horse with all the zeal of a kamikaze pilot on speed.

Some team, eh?

Kiborr doesn't have as much to do with the actual capture as Rutherfurd, but without him as a back-up man it would be an impossible undertaking. The technique used by Rutherfurd is this: he separates a baby from the herd, comes alongside it at a full gallop and slips a rope over its head, then lets go of the reins, leans over and gets his arm round its neck and wrestles it to the ground. If Rutherfurd wins, we have a giraffe. If the giraffe wins, we have a funeral. Assuming for the moment that Rutherfurd wins the first few seconds of the bout, Kiborr must then help him to rope it and hold it, because there is no way that he could hope to subdue a 450-pound wild and kicking giraffe by himself. (If either of them paused to consider what it is they do with such apparent nonchalance, they would undoubtedly dismount at once, lock the horses in the stable, and spend the morning with a cool/warm beer instead.)

Once a giraffe is roped, Kiborr's main job is to keep its head upright. If a giraffe lies prone or its head goes down for some reason, it dies in a matter of minutes from burst blood vessels in the brain. There is a special mechanism of valves in the long neck and a spongelike device at the back of the skull which permit a giraffe to lower its head to the ground to drink or to nibble something succulent, but it can maintain this position for only a very short period before it experiences mounting blood pressure in the head and jerks itself upright.

Now, as we readied ourselves for the great undertaking, Rick and Jock and I loaded the Land Rover with cameras and asked Rutherfurd if his equipment was ready. His "equipment" consisted of a rope noose suspended from a six-foot stick which he had just cut from a tree. He had tied the noose to the stick with pink embroidery thread in such a way that the rope ran down the handle and coiled in his hand. Rutherfurd does not know the skill of lassoing and so he uses the stick to slip the loop over the baby's head, whereupon the thread breaks with the tension, he drops the stick, and is left holding the other end of the rope.

They set off on the horses, we in the Land Rover, and within no time we were stuck in an ant-bear hole. Five minutes after pushing ourselves out we were in another. Then Rick tried walking in front of the Land Rover, pointing out holes so that Jock could dodge

24

them. Even so we went into yet another, until finally we abandoned the car and got out and walked, dragging our camera equipment with us. No more than a couple of miles from the farm buildings we spotted the group of giraffe which we had seen the evening before. They were standing on the far side of a swampy area.

We joined Rutherfurd, who had dismounted to check the girth before the chase, and I held his stick and rope while he did so. As I moved to hand him the equipment when he was ready, Douglas shied and broke loose, scared by a silly length of rope rather than by the real danger of giraffe or of ant-bear holes. For a moment it looked as if the whole operation would be aborted as Douglas danced around out of reach, but in the end Rutherfurd managed to grasp the hanging reins and we were back in the giraffe business.

Astride Douglas once more, Rutherfurd gripped his stick tightly and without a word set off towards the herd. Like a guided missile beamed onto a target aircraft, he concentrated on nothing else.

At first he approached the herd holding Douglas at a gentle walk, trying to get as close as possible before they started to move off. He was still a quarter of a mile away, and although the giraffe could see him they regarded him simply as passing traffic and were not yet frightened. In a minute, though, they stopped feeding and started to walk away, and as they did this he began to trot. He was able to trot for a hundred yards or so before they broke into their enormous, striding gallop.

The herd's technique to protect the babies is to get them out in front, and since they can run just as fast as their parents the whole herd is soon moving at a fantastic rate across the countryside, though it looks slower and more stately because of the enormous size of the animals. The horses seem like scurrying ants alongside. This is one of the hard parts for Rutherfurd (as if the rest were easy), and as we watch he attempts the only thing that will give the mission a chance of success: he must bore through the center of the herd amid flying hoofs and swerving animals in order to try to cut the target baby away from the others.

Rick and Jock and I are supposed to be filming now, but none of us even picks up a camera, we are so transfixed. Our hearts are pounding as Rutherfurd goes right into the center of the moving mass of giant animals so that it looks as if he is drowning in giraffe, who are running and kicking wildly. I tell you, it is the most exciting thing I have ever seen, much more than a bullfight, much more than Muhammad Ali at Madison Square Garden—I have never witnessed anything to approach it.

The reason this part is particularly horrendous is that the giraffe are fresh at this stage of the chase and their speed is like the final furlong of the Kentucky Derby. We lose Rutherfurd in the dust and confusion, and an enormous bull giraffe puts his foot into a hole and does a thirty-m.p.h. somersault and rolls back onto his feet. Then we see Rutherfurd emerge from the front of the herd, almost touching a baby. Having been got away from the herd, it must now be kept away, and Kiborr and Turbo (Jet) are vital to this part of the exercise, forcing it back into Rutherfurd's line every time it tries to swerve away.

The speed is still sickening, but after a mile now of going flat out the baby is starting to tire. Riveted, watching through binoculars, we now see Rutherfurd come alongside and reach out with his noose, which he hooks over the baby's head, but then the giraffe jerks sideways, catching the noose momentarily in one of its horns, and manages to shake free. Rutherfurd is now left with a rope but no stick, and we let our breath out. That's it for the day—a brave but abortive attempt.

Not a bit of it. The chase continues and we see, gazing spell-bound, that a new lease on life has come to the baby and they all disappear from our sight at full speed over the crest of a small hill.

We run towards the hill. I lose my shoes from time to time in patches of swampy mud, but finally we can see over the top. Not a sign of a giraffe or a horse anywhere. What has happened? Where is

everybody? Is anybody still alive? What the hell is going on? The emptiness is almost spookier than the chase. We haul ourselves, panting, back to the Land Rover and twenty minutes later have maneuvered it to a good vantage point. Rick stands on top for extra height and visibility and looks out over eighteen thousand acres. Nothing. I know they are all dead, giraffe, horses, men, piled up on top of one another in some little gully serving as a mass grave.

Finally, in the distance, we spot two horses. One riderless. I am certain the other person must be dead but can't see which is the survivor. Why did we ever start this mad escapade? The horses are coming slowly towards us, and, squinting through the binoculars now, I can see that the survivor is Rutherfurd. No Kiborr. We drive, weaving between ant-bear holes, to meet him, and as we get closer I can see that he looks drugged, as if it's a major effort even to sit astride the sweat-lathered horse. I know he will fall off and die in my arms.

"Hi," he says, casual as hell.

"Hi," we reply foolishly, "how are you?"

"Fine." Very cool.

"Where's the syce?" Afraid almost to ask.

"Over there." Nodding towards another hill.

"What's he doing?" I ask. (It sounded better than, "Is he dead?")

"He's holding the giraffe."

"*You got one!?*"

"Sure."

It had been a three-mile chase.

What had happened after they disappeared from sight was that the chase had gone on for more than a mile until Douglas, who was both older and stronger than the young giraffe, had managed to come alongside again, and at full gallop Rutherfurd let go of his reins and threw one arm around its neck while holding on to the pommel of the saddle with the other hand. With the giraffe still galloping and kicking, it had been up to Douglas to bring everything to a standstill.

Kiborr, arriving a few seconds later, jumped off his horse and with a length of rope rushed in to help as Rutherfurd threw the baby to the ground in the marshy spot where they had finally stopped. A long chase is bad for the youngsters, since they can become exhausted and die as a result. There is also a strong element of shock in the whole proceeding, and so Rutherfurd had taken his

28

shirt off immediately after the capture and covered the baby's head with it so that it could see nothing for ten minutes or so. (Personally I felt that this would make me even more panicky, but evidently it is not so with giraffe.)

There was nothing more that Rutherfurd and Kiborr could do then until we arrived with the vehicle to help, so he had come to look for us.

We followed him and Douglas back, winding our way through high grass and low bushes, every now and then crossing little paths made by the wild animals and the cattle. Reaching the top of a slight rise, we were able to look down over a marsh contained in a saucerlike depression about half a mile wide. We could still see nothing, but after picking our way across the soft ground for a hundred yards I followed Rutherfurd's pointing finger and could just make out Kiborr's head—and something else—through the reeds. As we approached, Kiborr looked around and grinned happily.

Looking at his prize, Rutherfurd said, "It's a girl!" Neither Jock nor I had given a thought to this question in all the excitement.

"It's a girl!" The phrase jerked me suddenly back to twenty-three years earlier, when my daughter was born. Little was I to know that the next time I would have a personal interest in the news would be about a beautiful brown-eyed, eight-foot-tall, 450-pound baby giraffe.

There she lay, uncomfortable and undignified in the short marshy grass, with one rear foot tied to the opposite front foot by a rope, and Kiborr straddled across her, struggling to hold her long neck upright.

Like all parents-to-be we had picked out names in advance, so we went up and introduced ourselves to Daisy Rothschild, telling her we were her new parents. For us it was love at first sight—we adored her instantly. She hated us.

Her enormous brown eyes glared at us in fright, and those long long eyelashes made her look like a very angry daisy indeed. We touched her; she was so soft—not coarse at all, but silky like a puppy. I kissed her nose, I kissed her on her head and patted her. Her little horns were tufted; they looked like two black paintbrushes sticking up out of her head. Her mane was a golden brown and shaped as perfectly as if it had been cut by Sassoon. Three brown butterfly-shaped spots ran down her beige neck in a row. Beautiful.

Douglas stood nearby, occasionally eying with a jaundiced look the tied-up bundle which had given him such a hard gallop. Then he started to graze. Turbo (Jet), unaccountably, decided that the whole business was too much for him (he should have thought about it sooner) and for the moment even forgot his beloved friend Douglas as he took off across the African plains. You could almost hear him saying to himself, "This here is one crazy place, and I'm heading *out*," and he was not to be seen again until later that evening when he showed up at the stables.

We now found ourselves confronted by a problem that none of us had anticipated. Because the chase had ended in the middle of soft marshy vlei it would not be possible to bring a vehicle to Daisy. We would somehow have to move her two or three hundred yards to drier ground. It was out of the question to carry her, so Rutherfurd said the only alternative was to get her on her feet again and walk her out.

Rick went back to get two more Africans to help, and the minibus. By the time he returned with them to the edge of the marsh

Rutherfurd had a detailed plan ready for the next part of the operation.

He and Kiborr slipped a rope over Daisy's neck while the rest of us formed a circle around her, then he untied her feet and let her stand up. That was when the fight began. We told her how much we loved her and she kicked us. It was like a bucking bronco and a bullfight all at the same time. Her back legs would fly alternately in

perfect precision, both backward and sideways with a scything motion, and her front feet would arch out at terrible speed with a forward and downward hooking punch, and none of us was about to get too close. Everyone hung on to the rope and grimaced and hoped. Rutherfurd remounted Douglas, as insurance in case she broke free and he had to start all over again. She would fight, then walk a few paces, then stop and stand quite still, neck arched— looking like a sea horse, and I was loving her more as every minute passed. Then she would repeat the cycle all over again, until little by little, over a period of about half an hour, we reached firm ground and brought up the minibus, from which the middle seat had been removed to make room on the flat floor.

It was an insane scene. There in the middle of the bush stood a Volkswagen bus with "Percival Tours" written on the side and six men trying to shove a giraffe into it. Rutherfurd threw her again, and somehow, amidst kicks that came sideways and backward and upward and downward, and by pulling and tugging and pushing, with everyone shouting at everyone else, they finally managed to get her into the minibus, where Rick and two other men sat on her, holding her down, and Kiborr held her head up.

Jock drove, and within twenty paces we were stuck deep in an ant-bear hole. Who would push to get us out? We were miles from help, with a fighting wild giraffe in the back of the minibus, and the only people capable of pushing were already fully involved in holding her. In the end, being the lightest, I was elected to drive, and Rick and Kiborr tried to hold her while the others rocked and pushed the goddam bus. I was a wreck, but it finally worked, and half an hour later we were back at the stables.

The help at the stables had "forgotten" to pad the stall earmarked for her with bales of hay, and there was much cursing and swearing as we frantically hauled the bales into the stall ourselves, while Daisy with her sitters on her sat in the bus. (Is that, perhaps, the origin of "baby-sitter"?)

All the while there was a huge bull—a huge *blind* bull, I may add—in the corral right in front of her stall, not chained or anything, but loose and snorting and pawing the ground angrily. That almost finished me. I kept asking, what about the bull? what about the bull? but they kept saying the hell with it, so I thought, O.K., the hell with it, and set up my movie camera and tripod uncomfortably close to it.

Then, just as they dragged Daisy out of the bus and she found her feet again, she took a terrific lunge and broke loose, heading straight for the high wooden fence. I happened to be between her and the fence with my camera and she came right at me. You've never seen anyone move with such alacrity as I did—and just in time, because she knocked the tripod to the ground and flew on towards the fence and tried to jump it. Unable to clear it, she nevertheless managed to straddle it, and there she was, suspended over the top of the fence with her front legs on the outside and her hindquarters still in the corral. Already scared, she now panicked more, her long slender legs becoming entangled in the railings as she fought to free herself and I knew she would break a bone and would have to be shot.

Rutherfurd and the team rushed to extricate her, climbing up on the fence beside her, grabbing the rope which was still around her neck, and pulling and pushing to get her disentangled. I could barely watch. Then she was back inside the corral again, all four legs miraculously in fine kicking shape, but this time she was under

33

control, outnumbered and overpowered, and Rutherfurd soon
steered her into the stall and closed the door.

The bull, being blind, missed all this but sensed that something
was not the same in his corral, with ten hollering men chasing one
terrified giraffe, and an hysterical woman falling about amid the
lunacy. He had been there for years, minding his own business, and

he couldn't grasp this new development at all. Now he stopped bellowing and kicking up dust with his front feet and stood stock still, trying to work out the anomaly of why, after all the racket, it was suddenly quiet. With Daisy in the stall, the clamor and activity had ended abruptly and I was actually aware of the cliché "a huge sigh of relief"—which came from everyone, even the bull. Most of those who had participated had cuts and bruises, but there had been no serious casualties—except perhaps for Daisy. Would she be all right?

Rutherfurd quietly gave us an assessment of the odds. His main worry was that he had overrun her in the chase. She had turned out to be a lot bigger, and therefore older, than he had gauged before cutting her away from the herd. If you catch them too young they can die from premature removal from their mother's milk, but if they are too old they have the stamina to gallop for three or four miles and in so doing can overstrain themselves, dying later of exhaustion. Between six and eight weeks is the optimum age, but Daisy, he guessed, might be twelve weeks or more—hence the difficulty in handling her. There was probably a thirty percent chance of her surviving until the next morning, he said, and if she were alive then, a sixty percent chance that she would get through the first forty-eight hours. Opening the top half of the stable door, I peeped in at her for what I hoped would not be the last time.

She stood in her stall—staring. It was painful to see her so frightened, and I wanted to open the door and let her join the herd once more, yet I knew that out there, because of the circumstances brought about by splitting up the ranch, she would not have even a thirty percent chance. Only the week before four giraffe had been killed because they had damaged crops, a fact which underscored the changes that we knew would soon affect all Daisy's relations.

Though I wanted to stay and comfort her, to tell her again that we loved her and that all would be well, Rutherfurd persuaded me that the best thing for her sake, rather than mine, would be to leave her alone for several hours to get used to her surroundings. The presence of the bull, another living creature just outside her door, would gradually reassure her. (*Reassure* her?) Suddenly overcome with weariness now that the drama was over, we made our way back to the cottage and collapsed with cold drinks and warm beer.

That evening we peeped in at her, but there was no change—she was just standing there, motionless, backed into the far corner, looking scared. We said good night and returned to the cottage. I fell asleep easily, tired with the emotional and physical strain. But I kept waking up worrying about Daisy, trying to convince myself that we really were justified in taking her from her mother and her friends, praying that she would survive the ordeal, willing her to live so that I would not have the burden of her death on my conscience. Rick said his conversation with himself as he went to sleep went like this:

"What did you do all weekend?" his Nairobi friends would ask.

"Killed a baby giraffe."

The next morning at dawn we got up and raced to the stables. She was standing in the same place, still looking frightened, but Rutherfurd was pleased and said she now had a reasonable chance *if* she drank within the next forty-eight hours.

For a young animal that has been used to suckling only from its own mother it is a tremendous transition not only to undergo the process of capture but to accept sustenance from a human holding out a pan of milk. We had padded the inside of the stall up to about six feet all around with bales of straw, and we took it in turns to sit there holding out the pan, warming up the contents on a little gas burner from time to time, and talking to her. Of course she didn't know what it was and didn't want anything to do with it. She looked even more bewildered and just stood eying us in a scared resentful fashion. By that evening, a day and a half had elapsed and she had still drunk or eaten nothing. By the end of the following day she would have to accept the milk or else she would die of dehydration and debility.

At dawn, once more, we cautiously opened the door of her stall. She was alive but looked bad: her formerly glossy coat was dull and she appeared listless, and sadness seemed to have replaced the fear. Up close I could see there was a tear in her eye—a real tear. In my state of guilt and worry, following another wakeful night, I imagined her asking, Where is the sun? Where are the trees and the golden plains? Who are all these strange creatures who do not look like giraffe at all and who keep poking strange-smelling things which I do not want in front of me? What has happened? Why can I not run in the sunshine and sleep near my mother and drink her good milk? Why has everyone left me? Must I stay in this dark place forever? I have never seen a place so small. Or shall I die?

I was sure she had chosen to die, and I did not blame her. Rutherfurd had told us, gently, that they often did decide to die, and no matter what we tried that long sorrowful morning she would not come to the milk. We even put a large rubber teat on a bottle and tried to drip milk from it onto her nose, but Rutherfurd said that we were probably wasting our time with it, and that if she was going to drink it would be from a pan. She now spent much time lying down, too listless even to get to her feet, and I knew the end would soon come.

More than forty-eight hours had already passed. Jock and I had the gloomiest lunch we've ever had together, and as we went back up to the stables to take what we felt might be our last look at her we felt hopeless and helpless and so terribly sad. We looked at each other, then opened the top half of her door. A tear, even bigger than the one we had seen earlier, dropped from her lower lid—and I felt one start in my eye too.

She looked at us, and then for no apparent reason she simply stood up and walked to the bowl of milk and put her face into it and drank! And drank! And drank! When she had finished she seemed so

37

surprised it was milk that she licked her mouth and nose and looked around. Then she took a step to where Jock was standing, looked at him, and bent down and kissed him—as if to thank him for the milk. From that moment on, Jock has been her mother.

We were ecstatic.

The moment signified another turning point too. It was her first movement towards us instead of away from us. Now, having broken the spell that had kept us apart, she came to investigate our hands, which we rested on a bale of hay just inside the bottom half of the stable door. She sniffed them cautiously, then put her head fairly close to ours, smelling us, then back to the hands again, but she would not let us touch her.

Four hours later we held the pan for her again, and this time she put her head in eagerly, gulping hungrily at the warm liquid. She didn't drink very gracefully—she didn't know how to. She would suck at it and sort of inhale it at the same time, like some berserk vacuum cleaner, and half the milk would be all over her nose and chin and the other half up her nostrils. This latter problem presented no great difficulty, because she snaked her long purple tongue out and stuck it up her nose, first one nostril, then the other, way up inside, cleaning out all the surplus milk. As for her milky chin, she ignored that, just letting it drip all over everybody. From time to time she would lift her head from the pan, spluttering and sneezing, spraying us thoroughly as if she were dispensing perfume in a department store. Since the milk was heavily laced with, among other things, cod-liver oil, in no time we stank of it terribly.

Now we had to keep the milk going for another few days so that she could build up sufficient strength and overcome her dehydration in order to be in shape for the 225-mile trip to Nairobi.

The next morning Daisy had her head out of the top half of the stable door, looking for more milk.

After her breakfast we picked for her some thorn-tree (acacia) branches which had yellow flowers blooming on them, and she recognized this staple food of giraffe right away and seemed delighted, but she would nibble only at the flowers, picking them out gingerly with her tongue from among the leaves and the thorns. Watching your baby giraffe eating yellow flowers is like watching a real live birthday card.

If she had been a boy we would have had to name her F.A.O. Schwartz, because she did look just like a stuffed toy, especially when standing bolt upright with her neck curved regally into an S. But "Daisy" fits her perfectly, too, because she does look like one, and she does actually smile. Really.

The fright had left her eyes now and she kissed Jock again. He could pat her nose, but that was enough for the present, and when he reached to stroke her neck she pulled away, reminded perhaps of the rope around it during the capture. We did not attempt to walk into the stall with her. To begin with, possibly for weeks, the friendship would have to expand on her terms at her pace, and we knew that to try to hurry the relationship along would have been to invite a severe kicking.

She was drinking four times a day now. On the third day, when we were sure that she would not refuse the milk, we decided that we would leave her with Kiborr and have a change of scene by taking a picnic lunch to an off-the-map spot Rutherfurd recommended, called Kaptarakwa, which is at the top of the steep western wall of the Great Rift Valley. We lunched on a jutting cliff which had a four-thousand-foot drop to the floor of the valley below, and a view that I won't even attempt to describe, because I could never do it justice. But take my word for it—it is incredible.

After lunch Rick casually tossed his cigarette over the edge and it blew back over our heads. He tried with the empty pack—same thing. Then we threw an unwanted sandwich over and *it* came back. Growing very bold, Jock threw his bush hat over and it soared up in the air, landing thirty paces behind us. Really into the game now, we flung the plastic picnic box (an expensive one) over the cliff, only to have it land in the grass behind us. Two little African boys appeared to see what was going on and we pitched them over and they . . . No, we didn't, really we didn't, but we did keep hurling more and more valuable things into the fantastic updraft, shrieking with laughter as we watched them safely returned. The odd part was that even three steps back from the edge of the cliff there seemed to be no wind at all. Soon two eagles appeared and they had a wonderful time, half closing their wings and diving straight down far below our cliff at what must have been a hundred miles an hour, then flattening out and being carried aloft a thousand feet above us—floating up and up at what looked like almost the same pace they had descended. I really wanted to be an eagle that day.

When we got back to the ranch everything was in great shape. Daisy had drunk and was peering out eagerly, looking for us and more milk (I'm not sure I have the order right). Douglas, watched admiringly by an infatuated Turbo (Jet), was prancing around like a circus horse, very pleased with himself and moving in a tight circle round the increasingly paranoid bull.

"He's getting bored—he wants to chase another giraffe," explained Rutherfurd. "He's feeling his oats, so I'll take him off them." He told us Douglas must be boss in any group. If another horse was even one pace in front of him he couldn't stand it, and he must run everything and everybody within ten minutes of any new situation—even the bull.

After Daisy's eight-o'clock feed that night we told Rutherfurd we'd walk the mile back to the cottage—it was such a star-filled night and it seemed a good way to end a perfect day. On the way the flashlight died, and I spent the rest of the fifteen-minute walk in the semi-blackness trying to decide if I'd rather be squeezed to death by a python or mauled by a leopard while Jock laughed at me. It was a tough choice, but in the end I opted for the leopard. There is something about pythons that just doesn't appeal to me. We saw neither one, but I did have to scrape something funny off the bottom of my shoes—python poop?

That evening we started packing up and preparing for the ride back to Nairobi the next day. Rick said it was a pity we couldn't drug Daisy for the journey, and Rutherfurd said again that giraffe, especially young ones, do not always respond safely to such drugs. I asked if someone would drug me. In fact, the thought of the 225-mile drive with her upset me so much that I decided to ride in Rutherfurd's car, which would follow the minibus.

At dawn as Rutherfurd drove up to the cottage, Rick called out, "Here comes our hero." It is nice to have a hero again—where have they all gone? Or is it just that psychiatrists have reduced courage and nobility with labels like "ego building" and "death wish"? Capturing a giraffe certainly never did anything for Rutherfurd's ego. First of all, very few (like three) people even knew about it, so not only was there no fame, there was not even recognition. Secondly, there was not a penny of money involved—he did it for its own sake, out of love of giraffe.

While older giraffe could be transported standing upright in a narrow crate, Rutherfurd had told us that a journey of over two hundred miles was too long for Daisy to stand up trying to balance, and that it would be much better to have her lying down. So, after lining the minibus with straw, we opened the door to her stall, and Rutherfurd and Kiborr, the two crazies (see, I'm as bad as the psychiatrists), led the rush of a band of half a dozen men to grab her. She reared up and struck out with a wicked left and right.

"Watch out! She could kill you!" I screamed.

"That's what she's trying to do," laughed Rutherfurd.

With front legs she chopped down and with back legs she lashed out, but somehow they managed to put the rope round her again and to get her out of the stall and alongside the waiting bus. Rutherfurd threw her, then they shoved until she was half sitting on the floor, but with her front feet still on the ground and her head out as well. More ropes round her feet, more pushing and grunting, and then she was in, with two men sitting on her and Kiborr holding her head. Finally we closed the door and spent another few minutes

41

getting her "comfortably" arranged and roped in such a way that Kiborr and Rick could manage her by themselves until we got to Nairobi. Rutherfurd had got banged up a bit, but the only thing he complained about was that he couldn't tell what time it was because his watch was covered in blood. Other than that everyone was smiling. Except Daisy.

Jock drove nonstop to Nairobi, and I worried about the nerve-racking trip they must be having with a fighting, frightened giraffe. Later he told me she was relaxed for most of the journey but had temper tantrums about every twenty miles, when she kicked and struggled so violently that he feared the bus might turn over. His main worry—and I'm glad he didn't tell me this until afterwards—was that the bus might break down and there we would be, miles from help, somewhere on the floor of the Great Rift Valley, with Daisy dying of prolonged confinement in the bus or, alternatively if we let her out, escaping and our not being able to retrieve her without Douglas and Turbo (Jet), in which case she would die of starvation.

At one point Jock drove into a gas station and said, "Fill it up." You can imagine the expression on the attendant's face when he saw a giraffe in there instead of tourists. Many Africans—and this may surprise you—have never seen wild animals other than an antelope or two, since the game on the whole doesn't live where people do. Thus Africans are intrigued when confronted with one of the larger species, especially when it is brought to them to be filled up with Extra.

After what seemed like an unending journey, we finally pulled into our driveway in Langata and parked near Daisy's stall, which we had built onto the end of the stables where Rick kept his polo ponies.

She seemed to have survived the trip all right, but you should have seen the inside of the minibus. As a result of her periodic kicking fits the leather seats were ripped, the interior trim hung in tattered shreds, and even the roof lining had gashes in it.

Rick opened the door while Shem, our cook, and the others who work for us stared with unbelieving eyes at the *twiga* (giraffe) that we had brought home. With their help we now slid Daisy out, trussed up as she was, onto the grass outside her new house.

With three people holding on to the neck rope in anticipation of yet another struggle, Rutherfurd cautiously removed her fetters. She just sat there, looking about but making no attempt to stand up. We talked to her and she looked at us in a bemused way and wouldn't move. We prodded her gently, but she simply didn't budge.

Fears rushed to my mind again. The trip had been too long for her—they had kept her head up all the way, but perhaps they shouldn't have kept her body down for five hours. After all the risk and effort of the capture, the worry of the first few days before she ate, then the joy of seeing her take the milk, were we now going to lose her? Five minutes passed, and Rutherfurd was just outlining a plan to hoist her forcibly to her feet, when she looked around again, then slowly and stiffly stood up and took a few very unsteady steps. Rutherfurd and Kiborr moved in behind her and she didn't even kick as they gave her a gentle shove into her house. They closed the door behind her and slipped the rope off her neck, and immediately she seemed to relax completely, accepting some milk and behaving as if the trip had never happened. I'm sure now that her not getting up must have been just a matter of stiffness or pins and needles.

Daisy had come to Nairobi from a relatively warm area of Kenya on what turned out to be the coldest night of the coldest week we had experienced in years. In the back of our car we found a tarpaulin which was torn and ragged and smelled of oil and gas and peanut butter, and we hung it in a corner of her stall in order to block some of the draft. Well, like Linus and his blanket, Daisy fell in love with it at once. To this day she rubs against it, hides behind it, peeks out from behind and around and over and even under it and is generally besotted by the awful tattered thing. Perhaps the motion of it swaying in the breeze makes her think of it as a living creature.

The stall we had made for her was built with three slatted sides, the end wall of the stable providing the fourth side. Half of the stall was covered by a high roof, with the remaining area open to the skies so that she could stand outside and enjoy the sunlight. It was a fine time, with Daisy just in her new house, to receive reports of a leopard in the area. A leopard could very easily kill a young giraffe and we had to quickly think of a means of leopard-proofing the part of the enclosure where she would sleep—the section under the roof.

So now she's going to be mauled to death by a leopard. There was little time remaining that day to do anything about this problem, so we stacked bales of hay inside her stall up to the roof and arranged for Rick's syce who takes care of the horses to sleep on a cot in the tackroom next door. The presence of a human would have a strong deterrent effect on a leopard, and if one were to approach, both the horses and Daisy would certainly smell it and give the alarm, whereupon a loud shout from the syce would scare the leopard away. We hoped.

There was nothing more that we could do and we figured that the worst was over—and, besides, now that we had spent five days with a giraffe and had overcome manifold difficulties we were experts. Jock, who grew up on a farm and had studied animal husbandry at agricultural college in England, figured he certainly knew what he was doing. He was wrong. The worst was yet to come, but at least we had a nice false sense of security that night.

Before turning in we sat down to enjoy a big bowl of hot soup on that cold night. It was only then that I remembered it was Thanksgiving Day, and I was suddenly saddened by the thought that in the excitement of the previous week I had forgotten to do anything about a turkey.

"Never mind," said Jock. "You may not have a turkey, but do you know anyone else who got a twiga for Thanksgiving?"

2

Everything's Coming Up Daisys

I hope Daisy slept better that night than I did. All night long I had mental funerals—visions of giraffe danced in my head, and dreams of a frostbitten Daisy whose eyelashes had turned to icicles as she huddled behind the tarpaulin to shelter from the blizzard alternated with pathetic pictures of her being held like a hot dog in a gigantic leopard's mouth as he gobbled her down for his Thanksgiving dinner.

Jock crept out of bed at 6 A.M. and came running back up the stairs at 6:05 A.M. to report that Daisy was fine, just splendid, sitting cozily behind her tarpaulin. I threw on jeans and a heavy sweater and hurried down to her stable with warm milk and loving words.

Have you ever lived with a giraffe? I guess that other than Rutherfurd and the Craigs and a few animal trappers, no one has outside of zoos. Aardvark to zebra pets, yes, and *everyone* has lions, *dahling,* but not giraffe—they are simply too difficult to raise.

There is an animal orphanage attached to Nairobi Game Park, populated by babies that have been found abandoned for one reason or another, which are then released when they are old enough. The staff there shook their heads when we asked how to raise a giraffe—very tricky—and everyone else we questioned who might conceivably know was gloomy about the prospects of doing it successfully.

When we first had the idea of acquiring Daisy we had to obtain the permission of the Game Department, and they sent out a vet and an ecologist to nose around our forest where Tom, Dick, and Harry live, and generally to check us out. Since she would not be a captive for long but would be released when we felt she was ready and would ultimately have to survive in the forest on her own, they wanted to be sure that there was enough of the right kind of vegetation around. There was—plenty of it—and they satisfied themselves that the land would "support giraffe," as they like to say. The vet warned us of the difficulties we would encounter in raising a baby, but told us that he was very glad to see that Jock and I were happy people and seemed to be happy with each other. At this point I began to feel that we were being assessed by an adoption agency, but he went on to explain that giraffe are very emotional and moody and get upset if people around them fight. (Stop hollering at me, Jock! You'll upset Daisy!)

David Hopcraft, another animal-buff friend, who is a doctor of zoology and has raised many wild animals but not giraffe, told us that with the best veterinary care and antibiotics and scientific feeding programs in the world, the most important ingredient is . . . (he coughed apologetically for being sentimental) love. He told us of a wildebeest (gnu) he had raised which had imprinted on a particular African and followed him everywhere. When the man had a day off, the wildebeest bellowed until he returned. Then he told us about a steinbok (a Bambi type of antelope which are extremely difficult to rear). One day, in an automobile repair shop in a village miles from anywhere, he had seen this baby steinbok hopping about the spare parts in the dirty garage. An African mechanic had found it abandoned and was feeding it. The next time he was in the area David made a point of stopping by, and there it was, much bigger, and skipping around outside among rusty axles and demolished cars. He was amazed, knowing how dicey they are to raise and having had many failures trying to do so himself, so he asked the man what he fed it. Far from having vitamins and calcium gluconate and sophisticated drugs, he learned, it simply got a little of whatever the mechanic happened to eat that day—sometimes a doughnut, sometimes a sandwich or some soup served to it in an old hubcap. The main point was that the mechanic loved his steinbok and it loved him, and that wild animals need love as much as food if they are to survive.

This advice was from a scientist with much practical experience, and you can be sure we listened intently. "They must relate to one person," David told us, "but you don't want to be that person—it is too time-consuming. You just want to be a herd member as far as Daisy is concerned." But it was too late—Jock was already Daisy's mother.

If a fortuneteller had told me that carrots were to become a Very Important part of my life I would have said she was crazy. I would have been wrong. Carrots are everywhere—on the bathroom floor, on the bedside table, in my makeup bag, on the windowsill in the hall, in every pocket, behind the sofa cushions, in the car. Suddenly life is filled with carrots.

During the three weeks we had had to wait for Rutherfurd to get Douglas and Turbo (Jet) oiled and greased and in shape for the capture, I had written to five different friends in New York asking them to please call the Bronx Zoo to find out what giraffe like to eat. I got tired of asking people in Kenya, because they'd always answer, "Thorn trees." We knew *that*, but I wanted to know some special goody like bubble gum or lollipops. I figured perhaps one of the five friends would actually take the trouble to do it, but again I was wrong—they all called and wrote back quickly with the answer. (Perhaps the zoo thought it was some kind of joke—five people calling in the space of a few days, or maybe even on the same day, asking what giraffe like for dessert.) The answer, they all wrote, was apples and carrots. Well, in Nairobi we can't even afford apples for ourselves ($3.50 a kilo), so we armed ourselves with carrots.

That first morning in Langata we gave Daisy a small slice of one, trying to buy her affection, and boy, did it work!

The first piece fell out of her mouth because she didn't know exactly what to do with it, but evidently she had sampled the flavor for a second before dropping it and wanted more. At Soy she had eaten yellow flowers, and finally the tiny acacia leaves, but she had obviously not experienced anything munchy before and was confused and delighted by the noise and the feel. The next slice I cut very thin so that it would more closely resemble a leaf, and she chomped on it in the most comic fashion—like a mechanical toy,

47

jiggling her whole head up and down to assist the chewing process, but you could see that she was pleased and intrigued. I gave her another piece, slightly bigger. She was getting the hang of it now—chewing as if she had been wound up, then holding her mouth open for more. I wasn't sure how to give it to her, and I held out the carrots as if I were handing her a nickel until Jock showed me how to offer it on the flat of my palm. You must remember, I wasn't the one who grew up around animals; I didn't even know how to give lump sugar to a horse. The flat-palm business was fairly easy for me to learn, but it took Daisy a little longer, and although she tried hard and was very gentle she would unwittingly catch me with her sharp teeth from time to time. Like a cow, she has only bottom teeth at the front; they are flat and even, but the forward edges are terribly sharp. I had scabby hands for weeks.

Daisy spent her first day at Langata consumed by curiosity. In fact, *most* of Daisy's days are spent that way, and if I had to choose one word to describe her personality it would be "curious." If I were allowed two words I'd say, "curious" and "gentle."

Everything absorbed her attention—her house, our house a hundred yards away, the stables, the horses, cars coming and going, the trees nearby, passing people, and each one of the neighborhood kids who came over, naturally, to meet her. She seemed frightened of nothing, just inquisitive, and stood with her neck arched and ears pricked forward, eyes concentrating intently. We were pleased, though, that she distinguished Jock and me from the masses and would not accept carrots or milk from anyone else. It made me feel important (and I love to feel important).

Giraffe have the largest brains, and are said to be the most intelligent, of the hoofed animals—which makes them smarter than horses. I don't know Daisy's I.Q., but I do know that by the time she was thirteen weeks old she was playing chess and reading Solzhenitsyn. Jock said, with all the pride of a new mother, "Daisy really *is* smart, you know. Today I wore my pink shirt instead of the blue ones she has always seen me in, and she knew me anyway!" I didn't think that was so smart—*I* know it's Jock when he has on a different shirt—but I didn't want to deflate his pride in Daisy.

Later that first day Jock drove into town and bought a large and expensive tarpaulin which would stretch over the uncovered part of her pen at night, rendering it leopard proof when battened down tightly and serving to cut the cold wind as well. It was hard to fit, and at one point Daisy somehow got underneath the tarpaulin in such a way that it was resting on her back and weighing her head down so that she seemed to be wearing a green ghost costume. I thought for sure it would panic her, but she didn't mind a bit and played happily, stooped over under the thing until we got it straightened out.

For the rest of the day until bedtime she never lay down but continued to be hugely interested in everything, as well as very affectionate towards us, coming up to kiss us through the railings whenever we were in reach. After dinner we sneaked back quietly to see what she was up to and found her lying down in the soft hay behind her Linus blanket, sound asleep.

Next morning at seven we rolled back the tarpaulin and gave Daisy her breakfast in the usual way by standing on the rails of one of the sides of her stall and leaning towards her with the pan. The

only time any person had stood next to her with no protecting rails or wall had been when she was captured and when she was manhandled in and out of the bus, and however affectionate she appeared through the rails we knew that we must proceed with care or risk being severely kicked. After three or four more days during which Daisy was occupied by everything, Jock climbed gently over the rails while holding out the milk, and she was so absorbed in drinking that she didn't seem to notice that by the time she had finished he was standing right next to her—or perhaps she did notice and wondered why he hadn't come in before. I had worried that Jock would be viciously attacked, but since she had paid no attention we judged it a great success as a first direct contact—a breakthrough. He repeated the performance at the three subsequent feeds that day, and the following morning I went in and sat on a bale of hay in a corner. She came up and smelled my jeans and shoes and hands, and investigated my shirt, and particularly my hair. Up to now we had let her approach us rather than the other way around, and she did so repeatedly, coming up to nuzzle us and to look for carrots, and within a week we were walking in and out at will, even turning our backs to her without fear. She had such a gentle disposition, yet the personality of a nice naughty kid came through at times. She was playful and just acted silly at unexpected moments, doing funny little skips or butting her beloved tarpaulin in some unexplained game.

Daisy, like all giraffe, being so long-legged and tall, has a hard time settling down into a sitting position and an even harder time getting up in a hurry. If the lurking leopard did wish to tackle Daisy, or a lion a wild giraffe, the way to do it would be to sneak up behind when they were sitting. Giraffe know that they are vulnerable when resting and unfold themselves into a standing position at the slightest hint of danger. Knowing this, we were delighted after about a week to realize that Daisy had actually allowed us to go right up to her and had taken food from our hands without getting to her feet. She was feeling very secure. So were we.

Following the plan we had worked out that would eventually lead to her complete release, we constructed a boma (corral) in front of her house. It is about ninety feet long and thirty feet wide, with a cluster of trees growing in the center, and more trees and bushes within reach over the fence at one end where it borders the forest.

We opened the door of her house and stood back outside the boma to watch. Daisy looked at the opening, then at us, uncertain what to do. Then she tiptoed out, very carefully, and gazed around. Gingerly, she sniffed at each tree, then turned away disdainfully and made a thorough exploration of the boma and the fence.

We were hoping to get her onto some other solid food, but carrots were all she was interested in. We had hoped she would like to browse off the trees in the boma, but she hated them—they were not the thorn trees she was used to. We had a few thorn trees in our garden, so we snapped off branches and offered them to her and she was delighted. After a couple of days of holding the branches for her for hours it got boring, so we tied them onto the branches of the trees she didn't like. We hoped it wouldn't damage her psyche when she was released—discovering that all trees were not necessarily what they appeared to be, coupled with the disillusionment of finding out that she had been conned. (I think it damaged my psyche, though. Can you imagine tying part of one tree to another kind of tree in order to trick a poor innocent baby giraffe?) As she stuck her head among the branches and cleverly separated the leaves from the wicked thorns with her long tongue and unbelievably soft, supple lips, she would close her eyes so that her lunch wouldn't poke her eyes out.

Our thorn trees were disappearing fast and soon we had to send Kiptanui, our gardener, sneaking around to our neighbor's property to filch Daisy fodder from their trees, and then, as that supply diminished and we ran the risk of detection (No, no, those nice Leslie-Melvilles—they wouldn't . . .), we sent Rick's syce out on one of the horses every morning to steal thorn branches from places further away, and Jock is ashamed to say it's still going on.

Every evening we would have "show time." It was Daisy's idea and she established the format herself. It would start with her peeking out, just like a kid, from behind the Linus tarpaulin hanging in her house, then ducking behind it and peeping again a few more times. Then she would come running out doing fancy kicks in all directions and take some fast spins around the boma before dashing back to hide again. At this point we would applaud by clapping loudly—even cheering a little if she had done it particularly well—whereupon she would peep out and do it all over again. Then she would have her milk and put herself to bed.

People are always saying, "Giraffe are so graceful." Isak Dinesen wrote of them as "giant speckled flowers, floating over the plains." Well, I've never seen anything as awkward as Daisy. When she runs she bumps into trees, bangs her head on the corner of her stall, trips over stones and stumps, and once even stepped right into her water bucket and got it caught on her foot. She doesn't care—she just bumbles happily around knocking into things with a bucket on her foot. Wouldn't you know we'd end up with a spastic giraffe?

During the first week the two horses were in a state of shock. Daisy was very happy with them, but they were terrified of her. The proximity of the horses was something we had planned all along because animals that run in herds, particularly, are used to the presence of other animals near them, and we hoped that having the horses next door to her would be comforting for Daisy. We suspected that the horses might be terrified of her at first, but Jock said they would get used to her in a little while (also they were not our horses). Within the next six months Rick was to get two more polo ponies. (I tease him and call him "my son the Aga Khan," but Kenya may just possibly be the last place on earth where you can play polo on a small budget. True, it's easier on a regular pony, but . . .) As each horse arrived it went into shock when it realized it was going to be living on the same block as a giraffe. Quicksilver, a beautifully trained gray pony, took one look at Daisy, panicked, and ran around in his fancy dressage gait, petrified. Then he'd just stand there staring at her as if he'd gone temporarily insane and was hallucinating. On his second night Quicksilver could no longer bear it and he broke out of his stable, but in order to escape from the paddock he would have had to pass close by Daisy's place and he just could not muster enough courage to do that. In the morning we found him huddled in the furthest corner of the paddock, where he had presumably spent most of a sleepless night.

Little by little, though, they all got used to the idea, if not to Daisy, and soon, when she wasn't looking and was at the far end of the boma, they were coming close enough to steal the hay from the bales which comprised part of the leopard proofing at one side of her house. So the horses ate her house and Shirley Brown ate her food. Just so a leopard didn't eat her.

Worried that Shirley Brown might be jealous of all the attention we lavished on Daisy—after all, she had been the Only One for eight years—we always saved three or four drops of Daisy's milk and gave it to Shirley Brown with much ado and great fussing. She thought this was pretty good, and whenever she could get away with it she would sneak into the tackroom, where we heated the milk, and would drink the whole gallon herself—which she thought was even better.

Every day we would get leopard reports, and each morning I held my breath while I waited to hear that Daisy had not been done in by one in the night. Then we would hurry down to the boma and feed her, and after each meal we'd play kissy-face—her way of thanking us—which consisted of a great wet slobbery face wash. After that she would put her tongue up her nose.

It is quite an experience to watch her swallow. Despite the length of their necks giraffe have only seven vertebrae, the same number as a human, but of course each vertebra is very elongated. No one has ever told us how many adam's apples they have, but Daisy looks as if she has seventy, and each time she swallows you can see the milk bumping rapidly over each one of them all the way down, giving the impression that there is some internal roller coaster built into her throat. Like cows, giraffe are ruminants and chew the cud by regurgitating a ball of it, and when Daisy is engaged in this pastime you can watch the roller coaster whizz down and up. It's hypnotizing. When she stops chewing for a moment, but hasn't yet reswallowed the ball of cud—this usually happens when she spots something moving in the distance and wants to concentrate on it intently—her cheeks get all puffed out like a chipmunk or like a kid with mumps.

One day when Jock was giving her her noonday milk, she nudged his thumb. He held it up and she took it into her mouth and began to suck it. She'd suck for about thirty seconds, then drink a few sips, then nudge his thumb again and suck once more. He sure is one funny-looking giraffe, she thought, and what a nutsy way to suckle, but all in all, she figured, it's O.K.—maybe even better, because she got more milk from him than she ever got from her giraffe mother. Thumb sucking became an important part of her daily routine, and she would also suck mine, and Rick's too. Sometimes I would sit in the boma next to her and read a book while she was resting, and from time to time I would stick my thumb out for her. She would take it into her mouth, and those huge, gorgeous eyes, framed by incredibly long eyelashes bursting around the edges like asterisks, would gaze at me and I would gaze right back, and I would know that it was impossible for anyone to love her more.

It did not take her long to develop a very definite personality. About three days, as a matter of fact. The first sign of this was one time when she felt she had not been given enough carrots. As I walked away after she had eaten every last one, she stamped, not just with one foot like an angry person, but with both front feet at

once. She also began asserting herself obnoxiously like this when she had finished her milk and still wanted more. And when she did not like something we gave her to eat she would turn her head away in haughty disdain as if we had offered her bad fish.

So her first days in Langata were a great success. She was happy with her new digs and her new parents and we were happy with her. Everything was coming up daisys.

I hate things to go *too* well, because I always know something bad has got to happen. Steinbeck said it another and more eloquent way: "I anticipate trouble because I don't anticipate trouble."

Daisy got sick.

When a young animal is suddenly deprived of its natural source of food, its mother's milk, there are a series of hurdles to surmount. If you can overcome the first phase of their not taking anything at all and get them to drink some milk, as we did, it is still highly unlikely that the new supply is the same as what the baby was receiving from its mother. We gave Daisy fresh cow's milk, with one third water, calcium phosphate, bone meal, multivitamin drops, multimineral salts, cod-liver oil, and glucose, all in a sterilized pan. It was worse than a baby's formula, but what we thought she needed.

Her system was now faced with digesting a new diet, and even adult human beings are not good at radical changes in that department—nobody is. We were to discover later that we should definitely have used homogenized milk from a supermarket rather than unpasteurized farm milk, because the latter contains much in the way of bacteria that, although harmless to a human, could transmit various farmyard complaints, the foremost of which is "scouring"—from which calves often suffer and can die.

Poor Daisy, therefore, *seemed* to be fine because she had something warm and filling in her stomach, but in actual fact she was getting infected by the milk and sicker every day. Jock was able to recognize subtle signs of her decline. Her shiny coat was beginning to separate and stand on end, or, in the words of horse people, it was "staring," and he said she stood "tucked up"—slightly hunched. Her personality was such that one might be forgiven for thinking there was nothing wrong, for she was full of fun and very friendly and continued to drink the milk eagerly. Each day I made an eleven-mile trip to a farmer friend to obtain the fresh milk for her specially, but, despite all the loving care, in the second week after she arrived in Langata her droppings told us she was sick. Concerned, we collected specimens, wrapped them in Saran Wrap, and whisked them to the Veterinary Laboratory for analysis. Scouring.

At that stage I didn't worry too much, because I didn't even know what "scouring" meant, and "diarrhea," Jock's definition, didn't sound very serious to me. Thank goodness he spared me the truth. He was very depressed and felt helpless in his efforts to halt the deterioration. Even though each bowl of milk, and there were still four a day, was now turned a light cherry pink by carefully measured amounts of Terramycin powder (the dose being based upon her weight, at which we could only guess), it did not seem to be curing her.

Jock made a list of all the vets who he thought might have had experience with wild animals, and visited eight of them over a period of two days and was told eight different things. Don't dilute the milk with water, said one, fortify it with powdered milk. Try keeping the fat right down and feeding her only skim milk, said another. The fat content of the milk of many wild animals, especially for the first couple of months after giving birth, is much higher than cow's milk, and you must boost up the fat, advised a third.

Daisy had started to eat cabbage as well as carrots, but one of the vets said we should not allow her to have too much moist vegetable material, though she could have as much dry lucerne hay as she liked. Another said she could eat carrots but not cabbage, and that she herself should have a built-in knowledge of eating only what would help her to get well. The cod-liver oil which you are putting into the milk is inhibiting the absorption of certain vitamins, and that may be causing the trouble, yet another vet told Jock.

Soon even I could see that Daisy was sick. She lay down much more than usual and I'd sit by her and she'd look at me with soft, sad eyes which seemed to say, "Help," and sometimes she'd suck my thumb, but even the carrots didn't make her get up. It was such a helpless feeling—there was no Dr. Spock, or even a mother or a girl friend to compare notes with. As with a baby, animals that are unwell are all the more pitiful because they can't explain what is wrong, where it hurts, and you get a feeling of being useless through being unable to communicate. Then Sam Ngethe, the African head of the animal orphanage, arrived to see Daisy, and when he saw she was sick he nodded and told me how his five-month-old orphaned giraffe had died in his arms, and how he had cried. We looked at Daisy and we both choked up.

When one of the vets telephoned to ask, very gently, if he could have Daisy's carcass for research if she died, that did it for me. "Carcass" is an even worse word than "corpse."

The next day Jock came back from a morning of making the rounds among the experts, looking relieved. "There are three people who seem to make more sense to me than any of the others, but none of them is a vet," he told me. One was Rutherfurd, to whom Jock had spoken on the telephone in Kitale, where he was returning Douglas and Turbo (Jet) to their base forty miles from Soy. The other was our friend John Seago, who is the most reputable and highly thought-of of the game trappers who supply zoos around the world. And the third was David Hopcraft. All, in essence, said the same thing: it was far more likely that we'd kill a wild animal by overfeeding it than by not giving it enough. David suggested we should get away from the farm milk, sterilize the pan meticulously after each feeding so as not to reinfect her, and cut the quantity in half. He said, "Milk me a giraffe and you won't get anything *like* the amount you've been feeding her a day." Then he asked, "Odd though it may sound in relation to a stomach upset, what about the love?"

Jock laughed and assured him we were not shortchanging Daisy in that department—indeed, he thought the danger was that Daisy might die of being smothered by love rather than from the lack of it.

When Jock told him about all the vets and their conflicting theories, David echoed something at which John Seago and Rutherfurd had also hinted: "Next time they tell you what to do, ask them how many giraffe they have raised."

And so we switched to pasteurized, homogenized milk, and cut her intake in half, and Daisy began to get better. And so did we.

We knew she was totally well again a few days later when she had eaten her ration of carrots and still wanted more, so, livid, she jumped up and down in the same spot over and over again—having a real temper tantrum like any other healthy, bad kid anywhere.

"O.K., she's fit again, thank goodness we're over that—nothing worse can happen now," we said. Well, those were mistaken words, but we didn't know it at the time, so we carried on.

Long before Daisy arrived in Langata we had wondered about the reaction of the boys—Tom, Dick, and Harry—to the presence of a youngster. Giraffe are not thought to be very strongly territorial, but even so the old males had enjoyed an exclusive run of the three hundred acres for maybe twenty years. And how would they react to

57

one another? Would the bulls resent the new intruder and try to drive her away, or would they welcome her, glad to have the light relief of a kid around after years of bachelor club? Daisy, for her part, might regard them in a number of ways. The sight of them could trigger a longing to escape, to run with them, or on the other hand it might mean nothing to her. After all, only a week or so earlier she had been running with dozens of wild giraffe, so what was so special about Tom, Dick, and Harry? And did young giraffe need to imprint on a mother figure? She appeared to have chosen Jock, but was this simply in desperation in the absence of any of her own kind and would the confrontation with other giraffe now upset this new equilibrium?

We didn't have to wait too long to get an indication. On her fourth night at Langata the syce, who was still sleeping in the tack-room adjoining her house, heard her moving around. Peeping out, he could see by moonlight that Tom and Harry had approached to within about ten paces of Daisy's boma and were very curious. She in turn stared at them but did not seem overly excited; and certainly next morning there was no change in her attitude towards her mother Jock. During the weeks that followed we were aware that the wild giraffe frequently came close to the boma and we specu-lated that they must talk to Daisy over the fence. It was to be almost four months before we found out what Daisy and the boys really thought of each other.

In about Daisy's third week in Langata I said to Jock, "Daisy doesn't like Kiptanui"—our gardener, who fed her from time to time so that we could go to the movies. Jock thought I was just saying that because I wanted her to like me better than anyone else (which I do), but then a few days later he noticed the same thing. Daisy would neither go up to Kiptanui nor nuzzle or kiss him, and so we left him gardening and hired someone else, who drew the same scorn from her. (We should have foreseen it—this one wore a cap with a swastika on it.) Then we put Tito—no, not the President of Yugoslavia, our other gardener—on the job, and he didn't fare much better, either. None had been anything but quiet and gentle towards her, but she definitely did not respond to them.

One day when Rutherfurd called to see how things were going, we mentioned the fact to him and he said, "I could have told you that before we even captured her, but I was afraid you would think I was a racist—I've never known a twiga to like an African."

It isn't Rutherfurd who is prejudiced—it's Daisy. No we haven't got a racist giraffe, it has nothing to do with race or color.

Intrigued, we watched very carefully over the next month and came to a tentative conclusion on this subject. Almost any hunter will confirm that wild animals seem to have an uncanny sense of detecting intention. A hunter on the lookout for something to shoot will find the animals jumpy and quick to flee, whereas if the same hunter goes for a casual walk unarmed, and not therefore radiating bad intentions, he will be able to get much closer without the animals running away. This has happened too often to those who have spent any time in the wilds for it to be simply a matter of coincidence. Similarly, in any game area in East Africa, you can observe antelope grazing happily very close to a pride of lion—if the lion have eaten recently and are not radiating hostility the antelope know it and are calm. Wild animals have a built-in antenna with which they can detect the intention of predators, of which the greatest is man. To say that any predator minding his own business transmits waves different from those of one who is in a killing mood is probably no more farfetched than, say, the homing instinct which carrier pigeons demonstrate more dramatically than any other animals, though probably all creatures have it to some degree.

Jock remembers his family selling a Jersey bull to a farmer and that after a week it was back, having walked sixty miles across deserted plains to get home. They returned it to the farmer and a week later it was back for the second time, and so they decided to keep it after all and returned the money. And think of those movies you've seen about cats and dogs walking around the world or from one end of Canada to the other to get home. Animals certainly retain faculties which humans have lost, and the detection of the right "vibes" (I hate that word) is surely an important part of their survival. Tiger moths can find each other by radio, and some insects have a chemical reaction to other insects which we have lost. (Or perhaps we haven't; perhaps that's the reason we like some strangers on sight and want to shove others down the elevator shaft.)

What kind of waves do you think Tito and Kiptanui and the swastika kid were giving to Daisy? They have barely enough money to buy their children a glass of milk every day, and here we were giving a gallon a day to a giraffe. I'd hate the damn giraffe, too.

The ordinary African has very little aesthetic appreciation of animals compared to a Westerner, and the reasons for this are not too hard to define. For those few Africans who do live adjacent to wild

59

animals they represent three things: they are a major nuisance if he is trying to grow crops, they are a good source of delicious protein if he can snare or spear one, and the larger and more aggressive animals are dangerous and to be regarded as enemies. (A fourth point has been added in recent times: viz., that a lot of money can be made from selling the horns and skins and teeth of certain animals, but we won't go into that here.) Most Africans can be said to have a completely different point of reference towards animals from that of most Westerners—valid and logical from their standpoint, and devoid of sentimentality. True, some of the nomadic tribes live intimately with their herds and presumably are fond of the cattle which they own and see every day, and indeed many ranchers and stock farmers will employ only men from such tribes, because of their inbuilt expertise. However, there is no reason to suppose that the relationship the nomads extend to their own herds (which represent their income and livelihood) is applied to the wild animals living just beyond.

We knew that Daisy's dislike of Africans had nothing to do with race or color, but we thought at first that perhaps it was a matter of instinct and that wild animals regard the African, who has always been around them, as simply another predator. But the fact that there are quite a few *individual* Africans—Kiborr, for instance, and our friend from the orphanage, who are truly excellent with all animals, wild and otherwise, destroys such arguments, so the matter of vibrations of intent, in the absence of any other good explanation, seems to be the most likely answer. If they can detect bad waves, equally they may detect positive or love waves, and that would bear out the love theory and account for the way in which the mechanic's steinbok thrived. (I must have been emanating waves of good intention ever since I was two years old and first encountered Animal Crackers. Are Animal Crackers still around—in those oblong boxes with the shoelace-type string for a handle? I hope so—I'd hate to think of America without Animal Crackers.)

Who, therefore, if not Tito or Kiptanui, would be Daisy's babysitter when we weren't there?

There are all kinds of unpredictable problems in having a giraffe. For instance, would you have thought that it would create fingernail difficulties? The first thing I had to do was cut my thumbnail short because Daisy's mother didn't have a fingernail on her teat and she didn't like mine when she sucked my thumb. Then there was the nail polish. As I held Daisy's pan of milk out to her one day she saw the orange things stuck to the ends of my fingers and thought they were carrot slices and tried to munch each nail, so I haven't been able to wear colored polish since. Giraffe putting Revlon nail polish out of business? Maybe that will be offset by Daisy giving a fillip to the lipstick trade, because she smears it all over my mouth when kissing me and I have to redo my lipstick a dozen times a day.

One thing I may market is a perfume called Giraffe Breath. Daisy's mouth feels like velvety feathers—it's soft like the tip of a puppy's ear—and her breath smells divine. Usually one says someone has indescribably bad breath, but hers is indescribably good. I've never been aware of anyone getting plus marks for breath before—I mean if you come up with zero breathwise you're a winner. I kiss Daisy all the time to try to define the scent; in the words of the perfumiers it would probably be "a sachet of roses and soft spices." I really would like to bottle it. I've never smelled anything like it before—possibly because I don't kiss too many people who eat only leaves.

So there I was, complaining about scabby hands and unpolished short nails, quite unaware that I would soon have three stitches in my palm—which I told you about in the beginning. As I said, I didn't know that baby animals thrust at the udder when suckling (and I'd be willing to bet you didn't either). Look, I couldn't even tell a goat from a sheep when I first arrived here, and I couldn't now if they didn't have tails. African goats and sheep do look alike in size and color, but I had to learn that goat tails go up and sheep tails go down; but then I couldn't remember which did which until finally Jock got embarrassed one day when I said in front of a friend of his, "Look at that goat," which was a sheep. He solved the problem by reminding me that I hate movies which have sheep in them and therefore I consider sheep a downer—so now I can tell a sheep from a goat. (The reason I don't like a movie with sheep in it is that you know it is going to be one of those lovely films which go on and on and on and on and nothing ever happens.)

I didn't want to keep having to go to the hospital—it would have become embarrassing—yet I hated not to let Daisy suck my thumb anymore. My husband the farmer settled the dilemma easily. "You don't think cows and giraffe get cut up by their kids suckling, do you? You must have had your hand against the fence as she sucked your thumb, and because it was rigid and there was no give, her teeth dug into your palm. If you let your hand float freely and ride with her thrusting it won't happen again." I wasn't convinced, but I tried it, and sure enough it works.

I am glad I married Jock—he is always helping me out in important difficulties about sheep, and thrusting. I glean all sorts of interesting items from him, such as that ducks can tell time very well. (Bet you didn't know that, either.) I am never quite sure what to make of this kind of information, but he always substantiates it heatedly if I look in the least quizzical. He told me that when he was a boy on the farm there were about a dozen pretty white ducks—Aylesbury ducks, he insisted (sometimes he tells me more than I want to know)—which spent their day on a pond, but which waddled up one side of the garden at exactly 4:25 P.M. every day to receive their food at 4:30 P.M. from the man who looked after them. And cows, Jock says, will assemble to be milked within five minutes of the correct time twice a day. And he also told me that on a farm in England once he was responsible for twelve hundred chickens, a thousand of whom committed suicide on a summer evening. It seems they were in a long open shed with wire netting at one end, and they started to congregate in a corner, piling on top of one another for no possible reason that he could see. Jock spent several desperate hours—there was no one else around to help him—breaking up the pile of living chickens and trying to get them to scatter themselves throughout their house where they had lived supposedly happy lives. In the end, he said, there was nothing he could do, because as fast as he pulled them off one another they jumped back onto the pile again and all those underneath were eventually squashed or suffocated.

Imagine being married to somebody who has been through a thing like that—it's not always easy.

It was Christmas-card time and when Jock saw what I had bought he said, "You're not really going to *send* those, are you?" They weren't Christmas cards at all, but ornate birth announcements which declared in terrible pink and gold writing, "It's a Girl!" Inside I filled in the requisite information:

> Name: Daisy Rothschild
> Weight: 450 lbs.
> Height: 8 ft. tall

and wrote "Merry Christmas" and sent it off to all our friends. It's not every Christmas you get a card like that.

Yes, the approach of Yuletide signified something else for us, too, since Jock and I were scheduled to give our first lecture of the season in the States early in January and we had to make plans to leave. We didn't want to go at all. Not only had our hearts gone out to Daisy but our minds had, too. I had never realized that wild animals could have such definite personalities. Her moods are mercurial: she sulks, laughs, plays, pouts, and has moments of ecstasy, is stroppy, confident, insecure, and shows many other facets of personality which would make a psychiatrist reel.

We dreamed of taking her with us and plotted ways to do so. To dodge the six months' quarantine imposed on hoofed animals entering the States, perhaps we could pretend one of us was blind and try taking her in as our Seeing Eye giraffe. To overcome the matter of headroom we would have to find a special plane that flew in a vertical instead of a horizontal attitude. Then, if we got her to New York, we knew there would be other problems: "Please carry your pet on escalator." "Curb your giraffe." No, we decided, it really wouldn't work.

Having no choice but to leave her, we gave the camera to Rick and told him to take pictures of anything extraordinary that might happen while we were away. "Extraordinary?" he asked. "You mean like Daisy lying on her back with all four legs stiff and up in the air?" I was by no means sure that was funny.

We also arranged for Rick's girl friend, Bryony, to be her babysitter when Rick was working, since Bryony was not only an animal lover but especially a Daisy Rothschild lover. Just to see how it would work out for Bryony, the day before we left we pretended we had already gone and didn't go down to Daisy's boma. She looked and looked in the direction of the house, searching for us, and when Bryony took her her milk she refused it for the first time. By noon when she finally realized we weren't coming at all she turned her back and stood with her tail between her legs (unhappy) and wouldn't look at the milk or Bryony or anyone else all day long.

You can imagine how that cheered us up as we left.

And on top of everything else, Rutherfurd was in jail.

3

The Animal Act

I wish I hadn't read the *Daily Nation*, our local newspaper, on the plane from Nairobi to London. There was an article entitled "Anthrax."

"Do giraffe get anthrax?" I asked Jock.

"Oh yes," he answered readily, "indeed they do. And they probably get contagious abortion as well. I've had that, you know." He looked quite proud. I waited, knowing that he would expand on that in a minute. "It's called Malta fever in humans, but it's the same sickness that makes cows abort—very nasty. That, rabies and psittacosis, which is parrot's disease, and anthrax are probably the most common diseases that humans can catch from animals, and there're about fifty others too."

Jock? An abortion? I sneaked a quick look at him, then glanced back at the anthrax article, initial unease giving way to something much worse. It read:

> In 1964 four elephants died of anthrax in a zoo. No one in the zoo had managed to diagnose the disease before-hand. The zoo officials therefore cut up the carcasses of the dead elephants and fed the meat to animals like jackals and cats in the zoo. They too died of anthrax.
>
> One of the people who had helped to cut up the body of one of the elephants also developed anthrax which started in the skin of his hands. . . . After direct contact, the anthrax germs enter the skin through some small injury. After two to five days a small pimple develops at the site of entry. The pimple rapidly develops into a large . . . 80% of those affected die."

I glanced at my small injury. So now I'm going to get anthrax. Charming. The New York doctor will think I'm crazy when I go to him with a small pimple on my hand.

"It's only a small pimple," he'll say.

"No," I'll insist, "It's anthrax. My baby giraffe was sucking my thumb and . . ." Next stop Bellevue. When I get my pimple I'll go to a vet instead—he may understand better.

A few nights after we arrived in New York we went to a Christmas dinner party at the home of our friends Miriam and Jack Paar in New Canaan, Connecticut, driving up with Tom Cochran, who used to produce Jack's TV talk show. The Paars are dog lovers, so I hoped to steer the conversation to a point where I could logically ask who their vet was and where he was located. I didn't want to come right out with the anthrax thing for fear of spreading alarm and spoiling their party by having them worry that they might catch it from me.

Everyone was intrigued with Daisy Rothschild. "What the hell's a Rothschild giraffe?" asked Jack Douglas (whose wolf was outside in his car).

Jock then launched into a long description which amounted roughly to this: There are three kinds of giraffe in Kenya, the Maasai (or spotted), the reticulated, and the Rothschild. There are many Maasai and reticulated, and then the rare Rothschild, of which only about 180 are left, all on the Craigs' ranch, but they wouldn't be able to stay there much longer.

Randy Paar asked, "Don't the Rothschilds have different horns or something?"

Jock explained that they differ from the others both in markings and in the fact that the males develop two small extra horns behind the main horns. Other male giraffe have two regular horns and a bony bump in the middle of their foreheads, so that one might say that they are three-horned and the Rothschild five-horned.

"Why won't they be able to stay where they are?" asked Jack Paar.

The Craigs' ranch, we explained, was being divided into ten-acre smallholdings for African families, and although giraffe and cattle are compatible—especially since giraffe feed off trees and don't compete for the grass—giraffe could certainly never live in harmony with farmers trying to grow crops. When the competition for land begins between man and animals, it is obviously not the people who are shot.

Miriam Paar asked, "Why the name Rothschild?"

"Because they're Jew-raffes," Sidney Carroll threw in.

We told them that a member of the well-known Rothschild family on a hunting expedition at the beginning of the century distinguished them from the other giraffe, but they had been known for years by a number of names including Baringo giraffe, after a nearby lake, and Cotton's giraffe, after another "discoverer." Finally they were officially registered as a subspecies called Rothschild on March 7, 1954.

"March seventh is my birthday," I said.

"Are there really no other Rothschild anywhere?" asked Randy Paar, disinterested in my birth date.

"Not in Kenya, but it's possible there may be a few left in Uganda," Jock told her, "but who knows what's happened there under Idi Amin?"

"So what can be done about it?" asked Jack, the only other person I know as curious as Daisy.

"Try to plan alternatives," said Jock, "and move some to a safe place. We got Daisy because among the many problems involved in capturing and moving wild animals is the fact that babies invariably become separated from their mothers and die for lack of milk unless there is a human to offer cow's milk."

"Are giraffe dangerous?" asked Peggy Cass.

"They can kill you, if that's what you mean," I told her. "Daisy Rothschild, killer giraffe. We have a sign up, 'Beware Giraffe,' and it isn't a joke. We were going to have our sign read 'Giraffe Drive Slowly,' and under it 'but then their cars aren't very fast,' but we were afraid people would take it only as a joke. Giraffe won't attack you, but if you happen to be on the receiving end of one of their defensive kicks, that's it—you're dead. One of the Rothschilds at Soy killed a man."

Jock continued, "Rutherfurd, the man who captured Daisy for us, was the one who found him and he said if a bulldozer had gone over the poor African's head it couldn't have done a more thorough job. Next to Cause of Death on the police report he wrote, 'Trodden on by giraffe,' and he entered the same thing on the workmen's compensation form and his widow collected."

"You could say it's more dangerous to have a giraffe than a pet lion," I told them, "even though a lion is potentially more fierce. I mean, you can tell when a lion is getting angry and it gives you some indication of what it may do, and also they can play rough games with you without putting their claws out. Although a giraffe is the most gentle-natured of all the wild animals, they are so playful—"

"And we could easily get in the way of a playful kick," Jock broke in, "that just happened, incidentally, to be lethal. There is no way to discipline a giraffe, and when something that big comes rushing at you to greet you affectionately and throws her front feet at you as a dog might, it's good-bye everybody."

Jock and I thought of ourselves as giraffe junkies, but feared that some people might regard us as giraffe bores. (Our friend Larry Ashmead, later to become our editor, had said when we first told him about Daisy, "You can have twenty minutes to talk about her—that's all you're allowed.") So I changed the subject and managed to get onto vets.

Jack and Miriam were very enthusiastic about their vet, claiming that he was easily the best in the world. Jack said that once he had had to treat a dog whose eye-lubricating mechanism had dried up. The poor creature was in great discomfort and so the vet performed an operation which connected its salivary glands to the appropriate eye-moistening vessels, and the dog was fine. The only problem was that every time it saw a bone or a bowl of enticing food it would cry. At the end of his story Jack wondered aloud, "If it saw a sad movie do you think it would get hungry?"

Dinner was announced and the long table looked most elegant and festive. Jack stood, raised his champagne glass, and gave a very warm Christmas toast. "I am surrounded by all my closest friends. It is a privilege and a joy for Miriam and Randy and me to be able to share this holiday season with you, and we wish you and yours all the best things that you wish for yourselves during the coming year. And, please, on your way out, stop in the kitchen and place your orders for Tupperware."

After dinner, unable to keep away from the subject of Daisy any longer, I took out a picture of her which I carry with all the care and enthusiasm that a sailor shows towards his Okinawan girl friend's, or a grandmother towards her latest grandson's, and everyone oohed and aahed and said we should write a book, make a TV film, create a full-length movie . . .

The previous night almost everyone present had watched a television documentary of a girl releasing orangutans in Borneo or somewhere, and there was a short but adorable sequence when the baby orangutans joined in a spaghetti feast, stuffing it into their mouths with their fingers and getting all tangled up in it. We confessed that we had been wondering how quickly Daisy could learn to roller-skate while smoking a cigarette, or get the knack of being dragged around a pool on water skis by a team of porpoises, since the spaghetti trick had already been done by somebody else. Jumping through an oval-shaped hoop was a possibility for her, Tom said, but an act by Daisy on high stilts would be truly mind-boggling. For a book title I suggested that perhaps we should change her name to something catchy, like Black Beauty, or entitle it Born Tall.

Peggy said that maybe she could come up with some ideas, since she had once been in a TV show with animals in it, which reminded me of the first time Peggy ever came to our house in Malindi, when she was on safari some years earlier. Dancy, our daughter, who was about eighteen at the time and old enough to know better, I thought, kept staring at Peggy and finally after half an hour asked, "Are you the chimpanzee's mother?" I felt it was very rude of my daughter to suggest that our guest looked like a chimpanzee's mother, but Peggy laughed and admitted that she certainly had been. I had never seen the show, but Dancy had been a faithful watcher when she was little and living in the States.

"Tell us your idea, Peggy," Jock asked her, "about getting Daisy to do adorable things."

"Well, first you get these two tall skinny people and a giraffe costume and . . ."

This was apropos of what she had told us about the chief chimpanzee who did all the particularly difficult tricks on the TV show and was in fact one Cha Cha Cha Morales, a Puerto Rican dwarf, in a very realistic costume. Well, they say it's great to be in show biz.

68

Jack Douglas, who wrote, among many other books, *The Neighbors Are Scaring My Wolf*, started to compare some of our problems with the ones he was having with his wolves (whom his wife, Reiko, doesn't like), but it was getting late, and June Carrol, an ardent Christian Scientist, exclaimed, "Hey, it's starting to snow—we'd better get back to New York." To which Jack Paar replied, "I thought Christian Scientists didn't believe in snow."

Jock and I were staying the night, and when the others had said their farewells and departed we settled down with Miriam and Randy and Jack to have a final Christmas nightcap. The curtains on the big picture windows were drawn back and we could see the snow falling among the fir trees outside, and as we sat by the fire with our old friends we were suffused with that wonderfully mellow feeling that can follow such an evening. The Paars have stayed with us in Kenya several times and Randy has twice spent part of the summer with us, so we were with people who have had much exposure to Africa, which relieved us from answering basic is-it-hot? and are-there-any-snakes? questions.

Jack lit a cigar and smiled at us, settling back into his chair. I could see from his expression that he had something important he wanted to ask. One of the reasons that he was so spectacularly successful as a talk-show host is that he *really* wants to know. He doesn't pull the questions out of the bag for any other reason than being a born interviewer, and his intense interest has the effect of making the other person enjoy talking. Now he said, "Okay, Jock and Betty—why *did* you two get a giraffe? I mean really, *why* did you when I've heard you say that you don't regard yourselves as animal people?"

He sat back with a smile, the master of provocative-question-without-offense, and took another puff on his cigar, waiting eagerly for the answer.

Having heard endless theories about the mental condition of animal people (bird-watchers may be sex sublimaters), we had examined ourselves in a lighthearted and kidding way, but nevertheless with an introspection that was real.

"My favorite species of animal is still man," I told him. "Mark Twain said there is no such thing as vulgarity, immorality, or war among animals, and that is true and very refreshing. But looking a little further there is no such thing as honor, nobility, music, literature, or art among animals either. But why do we have to choose? Why can't we have both man and giraffe? Naturally, if a child and a dog were both drowning anyone would save the child, but why can't we try to save both—people and animals?"

"And," added Jock, "like a van Gogh or a Michelangelo, a giraffe is a thing of beauty, and an animal species once extinct cannot be replaced—man cannot recreate them. We are not the only species to inhabit the earth, and what right have we to eliminate the others?"

"They must be saved," I said, "not only for their sake, but for our own sake too—for man's sake—because animals add such beauty and diversity to our lives. Circumstances have led us to saving giraffe. If we lived in Indian Head, New York, we'd probably be fighting nuclear power plants . . ." (As you can see we get quite carried away when talking to the Paars.)

Randy said, "I read that people give more money to the SPCA than to children. . . ."

Jock didn't let her get any further. "I think that is terrible too. *But* there are government agencies and laws to protect children, and who's ever heard of an abandoned child left on a doorstep that someone didn't take in?"

"And when they start clubbing six thousand babies to death every year, as they do the seals, we'll start hollering about them too," I added.

"Okay," said Jack, "let's not get onto seals. Let's stick to giraffe. Really, why did you get a giraffe when I've heard your theory that the most common pets, dogs and cats, are by far the most satisfactory animals for a human to keep—and that you definitely don't like the idea of wild animals as pets? You used to be just as adamant about that as you are now about having a wild animal."

"We still don't like the idea of wild pets," Jock answered, "because wild animals are wild, Jack, and a year or two of exposure to a human doesn't amount to the thousands of years that dogs and horses and cows have spent around man. There's probably no such thing as a tame wild animal. Tolerant, maybe, but not tame. We know of wild animal owners in Kenya who have been crushed by rhino, poisoned by snakes, put into hospital by wildebeest—it nearly always ends badly. Most monkeys make rotten pets because they're hard to housetrain, have unpleasant habits, and frequently become dangerously vicious as they get older. Birds, on the whole, don't respond too well, antelope will gore you as soon as look at you— they are far more dangerous than a pet lion—and alligators and things of that kind can hardly be said to be cuddly or companionable. Another reason that we are not in favor of people keeping wild animals is that the relationship so often ends in heartbreak or disaster—like your sad ending with Amani, who had to be the cutest lion cub we ever saw."

"You're right," said Miriam, "I don't think any of us has ever been so upset as when he had to go to Lion Country Safari in Florida, but the winter up here would have been just too cold for him."

"So why did you get a giraffe?" insisted Jack.

"For quite a few reasons," Jock answered. "One, we had to ask ourselves if we really cared about saving an endangered species, and the answer is yes, we really do. The situation was there—sort of thrust upon us—and we were in a position where we had the land to keep a giraffe, the education to understand the problem, and the time to devote to solve it. So how could we say no?"

"And, to be completely honest," I said, "on the personal level it pleased us—nothing wrong with that—I'm a great believer in pleasure. And perhaps we all have a need to be needed. . . ."

Jock interrupted, (we often take over from each other in midsentence, especially when talking about Africa—probably a hangover from lecturing together), "And being needed by an animal beats being needed by a person every time, because when looking after Grandma gets to be a pain, there's not much you can do about it. I mean you can't have her put down or give her to a zoo. With animals we have a choice. There are justifiable options: 'It's unfair to keep Rover cooped up in this apartment after he's run on the farm all his life,' or 'We're moving to Ontario and can't take the camel'—anything—but with Granny you're stuck, and when there's no route marked exit and you *have* to take care of her or go to jail for doing her in, that's when you begin to hate her and yourself and everyone else involved with the wretched situation. With an animal, since you can end the arrangement any time you want, you are more likely to choose continuing to care for the poor helpless thing. . . ."

". . . And doing so makes you appear kind, loving, magnificent—at least to yourself," I added. "What sometimes astonishes me are the conversations I hear about whether a Great Dane is smarter than an Irish setter. Would anyone get a dog for intellectual companionship? Jane Goodall told us her chimpanzee can count to four, but I have lots of friends who can count to forty—some even to four hundred."

"Animal lovers can't be all bad," Randy cut in.

"Of course not," answered Jock. "It's not what some of the re-

71

nowned animal lovers *do* with wild animals that bothers me, it's what they *think* about what they do that bothers me."

"You mean about keeping them captive?" asked Jack. "Or letting them go when they're big enough to take care of themselves?"

Now we were really getting down to the contentious guts of the subject, and Jack, sensing this, leaned forward in his chair. He had asked the loaded question and he knew it.

Jock and I readied ourselves.

Yes, at first glance, we explained, the release of a captive wild animal into its own natural environment is an automatic heart clutcher. Free at last, it will bound into the setting sun to join others of its own kind and to roam over the vast wilderness. No longer confined behind bars or cement moats, no longer a prisoner or a toy of man, it will find a life with a fairy-tale ending.

Alas, such is not necessarily the case. Most baby animals are easily able to zero in on an individual human who then becomes the mother figure (even though she may be Jock) while other humans whom it sees during the course of the day become herd members. Knowing no other life, the young animal makes its adjustments within the framework and can become perfectly "happy." Its friendship bonds and its security relate to people and to the surroundings in which it finds itself. An animal will get used to this kind of cushy life and grow to like it. Then all of a sudden its human "mother" puts it into a truck, drives it out to some wild place, and gives it a shove in the direction of the setting sun.

Panic.

The new place is unfamiliar, there are all kinds of strange smells drifting across the plains towards it, and it has no idea what is going on. The humans, sensitive to its confusion, stick around in a tent or cabin on the edge of the wilderness to give initial reassurance. Pathetically, it stays near them and is almost reluctant to fend for itself. Instead of having food supplied to it on a regular basis by friendly people, it is now expected to do something about that problem itself—and it may be very ill-equipped to cope, especially if it is a predator. Remember, no animal could be released in the wild until some time after it has been weaned from the usual diet of warm cow's milk provided by man. Its wild cousins of the same age have got to know each other in the meanwhile, and have been instructed both deliberately by their parents and through a process of osmosis in survival techniques.

Staying around the camp, constantly coming back to base,

72

though foraging ineptly for itself out of absolute necessity, the re-leasee adjusts a little to its new (natural?) environment. Gradually some timidity evaporates and it seems to be able to cope. However, one day it returns to camp to find that its "parents" have folded their tents and stolen away in the night. Something akin to desolation and abandonment must be felt as it wanders off morosely attempt-ing to join others of its kind. As far as the wild ones are concerned the newcomer does not conform in subtle ways and is an oddball to be rejected from the already established groups. In the case of many species with strong territorial instincts the newcomer finds himself on somebody else's territory no matter where he goes and is repeat-edly beaten up for being there.

The humans, meanwhile, return happily to the city convinced that they have done something wonderful.

Believing this to be nearer the true account of what happens than the storybook version, Jock and I told the Paars, we were filled with doubts at the beginning about having a pet wild animal which we would then release, especially since the best answer to the problem is for nobody to have wild animal pets in the first place so that the very question of release doesn't have to arise. However, the more we thought about it, the ingredients in our particular situation did seem different. There we were, on our fifteen acres with three hundred acres of virgin African forest immediately accessible, and beyond that lay the Kitengela, which is a vast plain filled with many wild animals, including giraffe. We had a permanent location next door to the wild area where Daisy could ultimately live. She would not be a captive, yet she would have our sustenance, both psycho-logically and in real terms of food, as long as she wanted it.

She would probably be like the rest of the kids, we told them, in that she would stay around all the time while she was young, then when she became a teen-ager she would stay out longer and later, until in the end she'd be gone for days at a time, coming over to see us once a week, maybe, eventually with her own children. We did not intend to force anything upon Daisy, and the initiative for a break, if ever there was to be one, would come from her. Her own house would remain standing, carrots and milk would be available as would strokes and kisses from us whenever she was in that mood.

Equally she could build new ties with Tom, Dick, and Harry and could learn about *la vie en girafe* at her own pace if she felt so inclined.

We confessed we would not know for years how this would work

73

out. Probably a gray and doddering Daisy would still be shuffling into her house every night thirty years from now to suck our thumbs and have some warm milk before going to bed, and if that were the case, it would be her choice.

"Either way," said Jack, seemingly pleased with our answer, "it will be up to her. Yes, I can see that."

Glancing at the clock, we rose to our feet. We had kept them up too late already.

"There's warm milk for Jock in the kitchen and carrots in the refrigerator for Betty," Jack called after us as we made our way to bed.

As we move from city to city on our annual lecture junkets we do television shows on countless local stations, and over the years in national programs we have been interviewed by Jack Paar on various shows and specials of his, by Barbara Walters on *The Today Show*, by David Frost, Merv Griffin, Mike Wallace, Betty White, and many others. This week Tom Cochran had arranged for us to do *The Mike Douglas Show*. So persistent is the thought among Americans that people living in Africa should be wildlife experts that we found ourselves involved in something which we hadn't bargained for.

Usually, this is what happens when you go on a big talk show: The approach is made to you two or three weeks before and a brief interview is conducted with someone on the staff of the show, not so much to find out what you are all about (they wouldn't have invited you unless they had an inkling) as to make notes for the host so that he can ask the most "interesting and humorous" questions. (What first gave you the idea of collecting nineteenth-century manhole covers? Does your doctor agree that belly dancing is the best postnatal exercise?) As a result of this process we are usually questioned about safaris, harrowing adventures, what will happen after Kenyatta's death (the temptation is to answer, "A State funeral followed by burial"), or what Swahili sounds like. That kind of thing.

However, at the last minute Mike Douglas' staff saw fit to have us cuddling two lion cubs and a caracal which they borrowed specially from Safariland in New Jersey. When we met them backstage about half an hour before going on, the two lions were snarling furiously because they had not been given their midday feed in order to be sure that they would hungrily attack the baby bottles of milk which we were to offer them on stage. The caracal was a really mean little bastard who bared his teeth and hissed viciously at us every time we looked into his box. I didn't even know if there were any caracals in Africa—in fact, to tell the truth, until that moment I had never heard the word. One of the lighting technicians nearby confessed that he thought a caracal was a tiny round boat used by primitive people. Before national television shows I always get nervous, and as a result bad-tempered, and this snarling little monster was just what I needed. First anthrax, and now this.

Really, we told the girl, we have plenty to say and we can say it without animals.

"Well, Mr. Douglas feels that it would make the spot more cute, and if you don't mind . . ."

We did mind.

Our perception of ourselves (have you ever noticed how seldom others actually share such perceptions?) has been that we present hard fact and serious information in a lighthearted and therefore digestible fashion. What we really believe is that our métier is with Margaret Mead, discussing the social eccentricities of remote African tribes, and we cannot imagine why William Buckley hasn't yet invited us to cross swords for an hour on the subject of African–American relations. How come, then, that we always find ourselves slotted somewhere just after the body builder with the sixty-two-inch chest has popped a hot-water bottle by blowing it up like a balloon? Never mind, I am getting away from the point.

It just so happened that our friend Virginia Kelly had been assigned to do a piece on Mike Douglas for *Reader's Digest*, so we rode together on the train from New York to Philadelphia, where the show is taped. She was going to stay around the show for several days, winding up with an interview with Mike, but for the first afternoon she planned simply to place herself in the audience to obtain her initial impressions as a member of the public.

Always at the beginning of these shows there is a rundown by someone who tells the audience about the "exciting guests" who will be appearing that day. We had been orally billed thus: "And, from Africa—Betty and Jock Leslie-Melville with lion cubs!" Other guests included José Feliciano, who was actually cohost, Al Martino, a Swedish rock group, and the widow of a baseball star. Right before our turn there was a commercial break, and as Virginia sat in the audience taking her notes the housewife sitting in front of her leaned across to her friend and said, "I think the animal act is next."

Meanwhile, behind the scenes we were making a last-ditch stand over the caracal. Jock told me later that he had run upstairs to borrow an encyclopedia from one of the staff members to find out something about the caracal in case Mike Douglas were to ask. Jock at least knew what a caracal is—the African version of a lynx—but confessed afterwards that he knew very little about their habits. Anyway, there it was, still snarling in its box, and even the handler was pointedly making no attempt to handle it.

"O.K., we'll take the lion cubs," we said grudgingly, "but no caracal."

They insisted.

"Then find another way to fill the next fifteen-minute spot on the show." If you are going to throw weight around like that it must be done with lean timing, and about fifty-four seconds before you are due to march out smiling to meet Mike Douglas amounts to perfect timing.

No caracal. Two lions.

Jock had one great advantage over me: he had paid attention while the handler was explaining how to hold the cub and what to do with the bottle. With his cub locked securely under one arm and its teeth clamped around the teat of the bottle, Jock strode out confident and smiling to greet Douglas as the last bar of the music of the commercial break was coming to an end. As I stepped in front of the cameras my cub, already in a mood as bad as mine, was alarmed by the sudden noise and the bright lights and stuck all ten claws into me at the same time, while taking a firm grip with his needle-sharp teeth on my thumb instead of the rubber teat because I had the bottle the wrong way round. I had chosen to wear a kind of cape arrangement with long flowing panels, one of which now became entwined around the cub, my wrist, and the bottle, and all this before I had even said hello to Douglas and sat down. My high resistance to pain, coupled with my even higher resistance to making an ass of myself, kept me from screaming, but my teeth were clenched tightly together as I mumbled something inane through them to Mike Douglas.

Then we were seated in our allotted chairs, with Jock looking charming and at ease and obviously bursting with fascinating information about Africa. Mike, therefore, turned to me with the first question, but I was having such a hard time I didn't even hear it and he had to repeat himself slowly. That's always a good beginning to an interview, when the interviewee is so dumb that she cannot understand what the nice man is asking. It came close to being the first time an adorable lion cub was strangled to death on live television. I

76

forget how the rest of the animal act went, though Jock assures me that we were awful. We took the train back with a deep feeling of failure, and my lacerated arm reminded me painfully for days afterwards about my public humiliation in front of twenty million viewers.

The day after the Douglas debacle (Mike, not the horse) we had a letter from Rick. Since arriving in the States we had telephoned Nairobi twice to see how Daisy was but had had the usual unsatisfactory aware-of-the-cost, O.K.-fine-how-are-you shouting-type conversations. Now in the letter we looked forward to solid, detailed news of her.

> At first, we feared that Daisy was going to die [Rick wrote], because far from eating, she wouldn't even turn around. She just stood there sulking, with her back to everyone all day long. Finally she came around (and turned around) but she is going through a *very difficult stage* and has begun kicking people. In fact she knocked Bryony flat just for the fun of it. For no apparent reason she lifted her back leg like a dog, and then whaaaap!—at a right angle, deadly accurate. Physically Bryony was unhurt, but mentally, well—I'm not too sure. Some friend of yours came by to see Daisy and said to Bryony, "Oh, so you're Daisy's nursemaid while they're away?" to which she replied, "No, I'm her servant."
>
> Now, we have been uncertain whether to tell you this or not, but we guess you should know. Ready? Daisy escaped . . .

"Jock!" I shouted, midsentence, "Daisy escaped!" He came running and the letter shook in my hand as I continued to read it aloud.

> . . . It was last Friday afternoon. We weren't there but Tito told us later that Daisy stood back and took a deliberate run at the fence, not trying to jump it but to break through it, and she succeeded. Once outside she investigated things and explored a little, then took a run just to stretch her legs and caught her neck in the wire clothes line which she didn't see, and it frightened her so much she took off and disappeared over the horizon into the woods. Bryony and I and Tito and Kiptanui all searched for her and we tried to track her, but in vain. She didn't come back all night, and all next day we searched and on Sunday morning we continued—really worried by now—but no trace of Daisy. Then on Sunday afternoon she came strolling up the lawn.
>
> She seemed extremely happy to see everyone again, and ran

around in *circles* when she saw her milk. Her escape has actually done her a lot of good because she is much nicer now—I guess she learned that it ain't so great out there in the big, cruel world, with no one to bring her milk or carrots, and so she is happy to be back sponging again.

Jock and I were weak—she might have been lost or poached or starved. We were glad she was back for her sake, we were glad for our sake, and we were especially glad for Rick and Bryony, who had been left in charge. I told Jock I bet they were two scared kids who had their telephone off the hook all weekend lest we should call again to see how Daisy was. "Daisy? Daisy? Oh, yeah, Daisy. . . . Well . . ."

They closed the letter by saying that Rutherfurd was out of jail. (Why had he been in jail? I'll never tell!)

4

Oopsie
Daisy

As soon as we were released from our U.S. lecture tour we raced back to Kenya to release Daisy. How we had missed her and how we longed to see her again.

When we had left Langata Daisy's head did not reach the top rail of her boma, and now as we swung into our driveway we saw she was resting her chin on it. Giraffe grow one eighth of an inch a day, and since we had been gone almost three months, she had shot up nearly a foot. The excitement of seeing her gripped us both as we approached her boma, wondering if she would remember us.

She did. Hurrying right up to us, she gave first Jock and then me a big slobbery kiss, then she ran around in a circle.

I had forgotten how almost unbearably beautiful she was. More like a merry-go-round giraffe than ever, she looked as if she had white eye shadow painted on her lids, and her lashes measured over

two inches long, while her S-shaped neck seemed arched in even more stately fashion than when we had left. She was truly regal, yet she maintained the sense of a fun creature too. Her butterfly patterns had become bigger butterflies still.

To please us, Bryony had taught her a trick—to take a carrot from her mouth. "Try it," she said, and when Daisy accepted a piece from me and then from Jock, but from no one else (other than Rick and Bryony), we knew for certain we were still loved.

Daisy had behaved much better since her escape, and never tried again, but Rick and Bryony said they were still not going into the boma with her, as she was inclined to kick, and if we got it in the head or the chest we could be seriously hurt or even killed. Something bad had evidently happened to her over Christmas.

Rick and Bryony had gone to the coast for a two-week holiday and had arranged for someone else to buy her milk. But the someone else left yet someone else in charge and the arrangement collapsed, leaving Daisy without responsible supervision. Luckily Rutherfurd arrived in Nairobi and came over to see how things were. He was told by a distressed Tito that Daisy had had no milk for a week,

80

and he guessed that she had probably had little food other than leaves, because Tito told him that there was no money with which to buy anything. Rutherfurd rushed off and returned with gallons of milk, calf-weaning food, and a couple of bales of lucerne hay. But what had Daisy suffered in the preceding week? And another thing: her tarpaulin (the large one, not her Linus blanket) had been stolen, all $150 worth. I find this easy to understand. A passing African might think, "One hundred fifty dollars to keep a *giraffe* dry? I've got better uses for it than that." Perhaps in stealing it the thieves had hurt her in some way. Africans often herd their cattle by throwing stones at them, and Rick has to watch his syce to keep him from throwing stones at the horses to move them out of the field. Possibly, being afraid, the thieves could have thrown logs of wood or rocks at Daisy to keep her away from them. Or something even worse. We will never know, but certainly over Christmas Daisy had developed a nasty streak, and though better by the time we saw her again she was by no means back to normal.

Rick suggested we devote a week to being with her intensively, giving her lots of love before we released her, so that she would want to come back into the boma after she was free.

So we spent the next week cuddling her.

Each morning she'd be resting her chin on the top rail, looking for us, waiting for us, then she'd drink her milk and suck our thumbs, and drink and suck, and suck and drink, then kiss us. Soon we could touch her face again and then scratch her ears and behind her tufted horns, but she would pull away when we tried to touch her neck or body. We usually wore our pink shirts because Jock says she likes them best of all (although how he's sure I don't quite know), and once when I was wearing a necklace of many-colored beads she tried to eat the orange ones, thinking they were carrots. Then she became intrigued with my hair and she'd chew it and chew it until I ended up looking like Topsy, because giraffe saliva is

just like Duco Cement (I wonder if it *is*?—must check the label next time). It hardens as it dries, leaving my hair standing in lengthy spikes. I hoped the saliva she spread all over my face with her tongue would act as a beautifying mask, since it felt like one, and we thought perhaps we could market it too—Giraffe Spittle Beauty Mask.

One night in New York we had sat around discussing the business possibilities of marketing Daisy Rothschild droppings. After Pet Rocks we figured anything was possible. One friend, a writer (who says he wants to be famous so he can wear his coat over his shoulders), suggested that we collect her droppings and put them into Lucite for the man who has everything. *Odongo*, which is the Swahili word for the mixture of cow dung and mud with which huts are plastered, appealed to everyone for the trade name: we would call it O-Dung-O, a product from the Turd World. Well, we had a lot of laughs that night, but the extraordinary thing was that when Jock and I returned to Nairobi my friend Doria Block told me there was an artist in Nairobi who was putting wild animal droppings into Lucite beads—would we save Daisy's for her? I thought Doria had somehow heard about our silly conversation in New York and was teasing me, but not at all—there really *is* a girl in Nairobi making giraffe-dropping necklaces and she had been doing so before our conversation. I didn't want to meet her, because it isn't nice to laugh when artists are serious about their work (and she *was*), but what astounded me when I saw one was how pretty the necklaces were. I loved them. After she has dried the droppings in the sun she paints them the natural colors of the animal—black and white stripes on zebra droppings, for example—then puts them into Lucite baubles which she strings together. For men she used a single bauble as a key ring. I was so taken with them that I did all my Christmas shopping, and it was only March. "What did you get for Christmas?" "Well, you see, this friend of mine has a giraffe and . . ."

Each day during our first week back Daisy grew calmer and more like her old sweet giraffe self. The four-month anniversary of our getting her was almost upon us and we decided that we would release her on that day.

I felt sad as I fed her that morning. Would this be the Last Breakfast? Would she take off over the horizon and never be seen again or would she trample us, leaving us maimed on the lawn? What if she went next door to a neighbor's house? Few people around knew we had her. I mean how would *you* feel if you were sitting in your living room and a damned giraffe walked in? Where would she be tonight, I wondered, and would I ever kiss a giraffe again? "Daisy, Daisy," I sang in her ear, "I'm half crazy, all for the love of you . . ." Yes, we had come to love her so much. She added such enchantment to our lives. But there was the rub—*our* lives. What about her life? That, after all, was the main thing to keep in mind.

So we made sure the clothesline was safely out of the way and we locked Shirley Brown in the bedroom just in case, but the indignity of this was too much for her and she leaned out of the second-floor window complaining about it.

There was no gate to the boma, though we fitted one later that day, so we had to dismantle the fence by knocking down a section of it with a huge mallet. When the opening was ready we stood back with our cameras and sang "Born Free." Daisy just stood there. She

wouldn't come out. We called, "Come on, Daisy, come on," over and over, but she wouldn't move. Finally we had to lure her out with carrots, and when she looked up and realized she was on new territory—free—she was full of wonder. She stood perfectly still and then gradually looked around, arching her neck rigidly in tense excitement. Standing, without moving her feet an inch, she was like a popped-up jack-in-the-box. Then she turned and looked at everything. After a few moments of this she cautiously took one step, then stopped and looked around again. Soon she took another step, then another, and walked slowly up to Jock and me and gave us both a little kiss. Very timidly she moved around the trees near the boma, smelling and tasting each one. When Jock and I carried the cameras to another position she followed us.

For the first two hours she stayed very close to the boma, investigating and sampling everything. Then, when Jock and I walked towards the house, she followed, and now she was on the open lawn.

With a little kick of delight she ran around in a small circle, then came up to us again. She followed us closer to the house, tasting everything along the way—the red flowers, the yellow flowers, the blue ones, succulents in the rock garden, the bamboo . . . with us praying, Please don't like that, oh no, not that kind, Daisy—noooo, not the gardenias. Like a kid at a birthday party she ate everything in sight—the popcorn, peanuts, ice cream, cake and candy. I told Jock I'd bet she'd throw up all night.

Daisy didn't have very good table manners yet, and sometimes she would get such a big bunch of grass or leaves in her mouth that she couldn't possibly handle so much at once and it would hang out untidily all around, and then she would jiggle her head up and down and back and forth, working her mouth and tongue to try to get the loose ends in—just as we all do eating spaghetti.

Then she spread her front legs as if to drink and lowered her head and ate the dirt. (Many animals do this, testing the soil for salt and minerals.) By now we were near our gravel drive. "She won't step on the gravel," Jock said as she stepped onto it. Then, spreading her front legs again, she picked up a piece of gravel, rolled it around in her mouth, and dropped it.

The warthogs arrived on the lower lawn—did I tell you we have a family of seven warthogs which also live on our property? Daisy watched them with great interest for about a half hour. Since we see the warthogs daily we were not as intrigued as she, and also it was nearing lunchtime, so we decided to let her stay with them while we ate. Not a bit of it. As we turned to go up to the house, she turned, too, and followed us. "She won't come up the steps," I said as Daisy followed nonchalantly up the steps as if giraffe walk up and down steps every day. "Well, she can't come into the house, she'll slip on the polish," I said, sounding like a surburban wife concerned about her floors but actually thinking about Daisy. By now we were at our front door, and Daisy was right behind us on the way into the house, too. The minute the door opened she put her head in and if we hadn't pushed her out and shut it she would definitely have walked right in . . . had a drink? lunch? coffee? We distracted her away from the door with a carrot and ran back into the house and looked out the window. She was peering at us, looking pitifully lost and upset that we weren't with her. So we took turns that day, eating in shifts, with Daisy looking in through the window between investigations of everything near the house, like the birdbath, the sundial, the flowerpots, and of course the daisies.

The excitement must have tired her, because as soon as we were both outside again she walked down the steps onto the open lawn and folded herself down to take a little rest. A small plane flew over very low; she ignored it. A car drove in, and she ignored that. But when Jock and I both went into the house she got to her feet and came running after us, up the steps again. We were definitely her security and she did not like being out there all alone. So for the next few hours we all just hung around together. Then, tired and thirsty, we ordered some tea, which was brought out and placed at the top of the front steps. This time Daisy was up the steps ahead of us—right after the tea. Whether she was just investigating something new or was thirsty, or was attracted by the bright colors of the new cups we weren't certain, but we grabbed them away from her even though we thought it would make good film. We could shoot it next day using our broken cups with no handles (we have lots of those). Shirley Brown was still crying, so we let her out and she promptly started to chase Daisy, the cause of her imprisonment. We yelled at her, since we didn't want either Daisy to take off or Shirley Brown to be kicked to death, and she stopped, then walked quietly

towards Daisy. Daisy moved carefully towards her and they stood looking at each other a few minutes, then Daisy spread her front legs and leaned down, and they touched noses and have been friends ever since.

By five o'clock Daisy seemed exhausted, and we certainly were, so Jock walked into the boma and she followed right behind him, most relieved to get back inside.

It had to have been one of my favorite days ever. It was an odd feeling to know that we had done something no one else in the world had done that day. With other important events in life—getting married, having a baby, dying—you know that hundreds of thousands of others are doing the same thing, too, but I felt sure that Jock and I alone had spent the day releasing our baby giraffe.

The following days were almost carbon copies of the first. The Christ's-thorn diminished, the blue flowers went, and thus ended the little thorn trees we had planted six months earlier. Everyone else we know has trees and shrubs that grow, but ours get smaller every day. Were we the kind of people who name their house, we could call ours Shrinking Trees Estate.

eck and neck

nes III, a 5-day-old giraffe, stayed close to his mother, Petunia, as tographers clicked away Wednesday at the Bronx Zoo in New k. James, named for a benefactor of the zoo, stood 6 feet tall and ghed 125 pounds at birth.

Sudanese protesters clash with police

Associated Press

Khartoum, Sudan
Police fired warning shots and threw teargas grenades at thousands of students marching Wednesday to protest President Gaafar Nimeiri's austere economic measures.

There were no reports of injuries during the march through the center of Khartoum in a third day of protests.

U.S. Embassy sources said Sen. Charles Percy, R-Ill., who heads the Senate Foreign Relations Committee, met Sudanese officials and Western diplomats as scheduled despite the unrest. Percy arrived in the central African nation early yesterday after visits to Israel, Jordan and Egypt.

The 4,000 students chanted protests against the United States, the Nimeiri government and the Washington-based International Monetary Fund, which demanded the austerity program in return for a $225 million loan now being negotiated, Western diplomats said.

Daisy stuck very close to us all the time, and she would not explore any new corner of the garden without either Jock or me to introduce her to it. Nor was there the slightest trouble over getting her back into her boma for the night. In fact, it was the other way round, with Daisy wanting to put herself to bed while we felt that she should still be playing outside.

One afternoon the following week we had to leave her for three hours because we had some business to attend to in Nairobi. When we got back Tito told us she had not moved—she had just stood in one spot the whole time in the hot sun, as if she were planted and growing there. She was so happy to see us come back that she ran up to the car and kissed us before we had time to alight.

It was sad really. If only she had someone to play with.

Tom, Dick, and Harry had not yet appeared since her *uhuru* (freedom). What would she do when they did? Were people her friends now? Were we her family? Or would she go off with the wild giraffe? We had to wait only a little while longer to find out.

In the meanwhile, though, we were to witness the beginning of a new trend—or perhaps the extension of playtime. Jock, Shirley Brown, and I had set out on our evening walk through the forest, and we had barely left the garden when I heard a sound behind me and looked back.

"Here comes . . ."

"Don't be silly," Jock said, "giraffe don't go for walks."

And so started Daisy's walks with us. No matter where we went, she followed. Once or twice we have really astonished people who are cutting through our property on their way home or, more likely, on their way to or from the Honolulu Bar across the river. They see a *mzungu* (white man), his wife and dog—a typical scene—but then they see a giraffe tagging along and it brings them to an immediate halt, and not a few rush back to the Honolulu Bar, I'm sure.

The first week or so of these walks was fine and the whole bizarre idea of it thrilled me, but from the start Jock wasn't as enthusiastic about it as I was. The point that worried him was, would Daisy ever take a walk by herself? She showed no inclination to explore our adjacent forest without his taking her there. He would lead her into the forest and actually point out a tree and say, "Eat that, Daisy." (He knows what she will like and what is acceptable giraffe fare through having watched Tom, Dick, and Harry.) She would chew happily on the leaves, as any proper giraffe should, as long as Jock

89

stood nearby, but she wouldn't stay there alone. Bored after a few hours of this he would try to tiptoe away, hoping that she would stay and eat her fill, but the minute she found that he had gone she would panic and come careering out of the forest at full gallop, looking for him desperately. If he was busy doing something in a corner of the garden she would go over and watch or nibble from a nearby tree, but if she couldn't find him she would stay around near the house, peeping in through the windows to see if she could spot him; and if that failed she would go and stand on her special spot on the lawn and wait.

All of this was very endearing, but in the light of releasing Daisy and preparing her to fend for herself it was something of a problem and presented to Jock a responsibility that he had not anticipated. Supplying food and shelter and a base was one thing, but being the object of such a strong need was quite another matter. Although finding it a boost to his ego, Jock felt burdened by this element of pathetic reliance so strong that Daisy barely functioned without him.

Early one morning the following week when Jock went down to say good morning to Daisy, Tito told him that Tom, Dick, and Harry had been close to the boma at dawn, and that Big Dick was still nearby in the forest.

After Daisy had had her breakfast Jock let her out and walked her parallel to an old dry stone wall down the open field to a point opposite where he estimated Dick to be in the forest, and, as if the whole thing had been set up, within thirty seconds Dick poked his

head around a tree and came right up to the wall on the forest side. Jock was standing under a tree stroking Daisy's face and was closer to Dick than he had ever been—about twenty yards. (Normally, the fleeing distance of a wild giraffe is around ninety yards from a man on foot, or fifty yards from a car. This means that as you approach they will keep approximately that distance between you and them, never letting you get any nearer.) At that moment Tom and Harry stuck their heads out of the forest further down the wall. Then they walked through a gap and stood in the field watching Jock and Daisy and Dick. Jock remained perfectly still and allowed whatever was going to develop to develop.

For two or three minutes nothing happened at all. Dick then started chewing his cud—usually a sign of contentment—demonstrating at the very least an absence of nerves, and Daisy began to pluck leaves above Jock's head. Then she stopped and eyed Dick very carefully. Slowly she walked to the wall, where she leaned over and picked a couple of mouthfuls of leaves from a low bush, still eying him. She was now only two yards from Dick, who had again stopped chewing his cud and was watching her intently. Lowering his head—he was twice as tall—he reached down to sniff her and they rubbed noses gently for a few seconds before he turned and ambled off into the forest.

The other two had watched this little exchange with apparent fascination, and to Jock's surprise they now approached Daisy, who was still only ten paces from where he stood. The fact that they had observed Daisy talking to Jock, even touching him with impunity, seemed to give them a confidence they had never shown before. Tom held back a bit, but Harry kept on coming, and then Daisy started to move towards him. They met, maybe twenty yards from Jock in the open field, and for the second time within a matter of minutes he found himself standing far closer to the giant animals than he had ever been—obviously due to Daisy's endorsement of him. Now Jock was able to see an encounter between Daisy and a wild giraffe when they were not separated by the fence of the boma or by the wall, but when they stood in open ground, each having moved towards the other.

Daisy looked so tiny. Her head barely came up to his chest.

This was the moment, Jock felt sure, when if the males were going to reject Daisy or punish her for trespassing on their territory it would happen. Many animals, horses and cows among them, will sniff a new arrival cautiously and then suddenly in a clatter of hoofs

92

and horns will turn upon him to show that they are the incumbents. Would this now happen? Would one of those massive hoofs lash out and knock poor, gentle, unsuspecting Daisy to the ground? Jock held his breath, and for maybe fifteen seconds Harry just stood there towering over the tiny nine-foot figure. Then, very gently, he lowered his head and sniffed Daisy. He straightened up once more and looked around before bending to touch her face and nuzzle her. They stood like that for maybe a minute, then Harry quietly turned away and moved off towards Tom. Then another surprise: Larry and Mo suddenly appeared just behind Tom, and they too had evidently been watching the encounter. Not only had they witnessed Harry talking to Daisy, but Jock was sure that his own proximity to the meeting had not gone unobserved, thus establishing him as an evidently harmless enigma with five of the six wild giraffe.

The meeting over, Daisy now had a choice: to move off into the forest with the old bulls or return to us.

This was when I arrived on the scene, having been summoned to the encounter by Tito, who had been watching the proceedings from the house 150 yards from where it had all taken place. The old wild bulls stopped and turned around to Daisy as if to say, "You coming?" Daisy looked at them for a few seconds, then ran and hid behind Jock, like any child with its mother in a scary new encounter.

Afterwards we came to the conclusion that Daisy would probably not even have gone up to them had Jock not led her in their direction.

On April Fool's Day Daisy went swimming twice—for the first and last times, we hope. We had had lunch, and Jock and I were sitting at the edge of the garden near a large abandoned fishpond which we were attempting to revive. It was a smooth, irregularly shaped cement saucer, about three feet deep at the center and about thirty feet wide, with gently sloping sides, and we had filled it from a hose pipe to see if it would hold water. We sat under a nearby tree lazily throwing twigs for Shirley Brown, who does not actually need that excuse to swim, since she will enter any water uninvited—including the fountain outside the Plaza Hotel in New York, the waterfalls on Fifty-fifth Street, various other fountains along Park Avenue in the region of the Seagram Building, and once a brave attempt on an aquarium in a hotel lobby in Mombasa which we won't mention further.

93

From the far side of the garden Daisy spotted us and ambled over—it would never do to be left out of any action, or in this case inaction. She came sniffing around, and with her feet on the grass near the edge of the pond she spread her front legs wide in order to be able to reach down and sip the water. (Nobody seems to know how much giraffe need to drink; we have heard estimates ranging from one gallon each day in very hot weather to none at all for weeks on end like a camel, regardless of temperature. Since Daisy is still having about a gallon of milk a day, we are in no position to contribute anything of value [yet] to expand the knowledge of the eager millions waiting expectantly for definitive reports on the consumption of liquid by *Giraffa camelopardalis*. Never fear, though— when we know we'll let you know. Look for it in the monthly publication we are planning, *National Giraffic*.)

Daisy just could not reach in over the lip of the pond. At the very moment Jock said, "I hope she won't go in, will she? She could slip on that cement," and I was assuring him that she wouldn't, she took her first step into the water.

She was ankle deep before she fell the first time, and she went down with a tremendous thud and a splash which drenched us. It was sudden, and surprising, and horrifying because she fell so hard. Immediately she scrambled to her feet and slipped again, falling equally hard and away from us this time. We leaped up and she tried to come towards us, which happened to be up the steepest slope of the pond, and she fell yet again, this time into the deep part, submerging herself entirely. I was shouting, "Do something!" but Jock knew that any interference like plunging in to help her would only be interpreted as an attack, and in any event there was no chance of being able to prop up a nine-foot, seven-hundred-pound giraffe that couldn't keep its footing.

She was panicking now. The relatively flat floor of the pool presented no problem, but every time she took a step up the sloping sides she would slip and fall again, and so heavily that we were terrified she would break both her delicate front legs.

Always marvelous in a crisis, I was screaming and crying, and the tension of such a moment is transmitted with such force by those watching as well as by those involved that Shirley Brown was frozen in one spot, trembling violently. Then Daisy was on her feet again and she stood stock still in one place for about fifteen seconds. Very slowly, and speaking to her softly, Jock walked towards the gentlest slope, the only point where she might possibly be able to make it.

Standing on the bank, he called to her, and she took two or three calculated steps towards him and got almost to the edge, but slipped yet again. I cried louder—sure now all four legs were broken. She was terrified and hurt and thoroughly soaked from the splashing. Then, from a half-kneeling position, she reached forward and got her front feet into the soft ground surrounding the pond and tried to pull herself out, but, without leverage from her back feet, which were slipping as wildly as ever, she could not make it. It was one of the worst things I have ever witnessed. Finally, slowly, while we watched in agony, she pulled herself forward to a position where her front toes were gripping the earth beyond the cement rim, and her knees slowly came forward so that she was kneeling on the grass but with her hindquarters still thrashing helplessly in the pond. She held this position and then, very cautiously—it seemed like a conscious act of thinking it out—she brought one rear foot forward until it too gripped the edge of the pond, then the other, and there she was in an amazing squatting-*cum*-kneeling position on the very edge. With the mesmerizing slowness of a circus balancing act she unfolded herself and stood on dry ground again.

She was dripping and trembling. Had she not made it that time, Jock said later, his plan was to fetch the long Persian runner from the hallway, which he would have draped into the pond and up the side in the hope that the carpet would give her the purchase she needed.

She took a couple of steps towards Jock and appeared to be walking all right—though I could hardly believe it. While I ran inside to heat up some milk for her, wondering if I should put brandy in it, Jock took a carrot from his pocket and held it towards her and she came up and ate it within a matter of seconds of getting out, and just stood there in the sun munching happily and drying out. When I returned with the milk she drank every last drop with such relish that I wondered if she wouldn't even go back and do her pond act again for another pan.

Jock and I and Shirley Brown were still in a state of shock, but Daisy seemed quite unconcerned and strolled off across the lawn as if that kind of thing happened every day. She has been near the pond many times since and has sniffed at the edges but has made no attempt to go swimming again. Months later another incident involving the fishpond would prove to us that she was not quite so unconcerned as she pretended.

We noted three things from the fishpond saga. First, she had been able to take apparently tremendously heavy falls on a really hard surface without injuring herself in the slightest. Second, after the initial thrashing around and panic, she had pulled herself together and quietly assessed how she was going to make her exit. Third, within seconds of her escaping from the predicament, her demeanor had returned to normal—much faster than ours.

We can do without any more swimming parties.

In fact, a few days later I felt we could do without any more walking parties either.

For Daisy, familiarity bred security, and security manifested itself in not simply being content to saunter along behind us as she had done at the beginning, in the way that animals on walks are meant to, but in proceeding from point to point in a series of flat-out gallops which were terrifying to anyone on the receiving end of them. We'd walk fifty paces or so, while Daisy watched, then she would do this frantic dash to catch up and would aim herself straight at us so that if we didn't get behind a tree we would be mown down. The end of each charge culminated about ten yards beyond us, and she would stand there stripping leaves off branches until we had gone another fifty paces and the whole business started all over again. From her point of view the charge was pure fun, and the affectionate thing that young giraffe do in the wilds with others of their own age is to knock into them—which is fine if you happen to be a giraffe.

People who are dealing with wild animals, even though the animals may be "tame," are exposing themselves to a certain risk which is dependent on the animal's ability to injure or kill if it decides to. It seems unlikely you could be hurt by your angry white mouse no matter how determined it might be, whereas even a minor transgression by a fully grown elephant could mean the end of you.

Jock told me, "She wouldn't run at you and bump into you if she didn't like you so much."

"I wish she hated me."

"Betty, you're lucky. There're plenty of trees around in almost whichever direction we walk and it's possible, by being circumspect, to calculate whether the next tree is in reach before the beginning of another Daisy rush." However, I didn't feel so lucky—especially that evening when she ran after me and caught me with a kick, fortunately a light one, before I got to the next designated tree. I admit it was a playful swipe, but a gentle playful swipe by a giraffe can kill you, for God's sake.

"She is only playing," Jock insisted.

"I don't care whether she kicks me to death in play or kicks me to death in earnest—it's the death part I don't like. Look, I have no intention of going the way Diane Hartley went, killed by her pet lion, or that other guy whose tame eland impaled him to a tree, skewering him to death."

"It would be more exotic than dying of lung cancer," he remarked in a nasty reference to my smoking.

"You know how I loathe physical danger. I won't even play tennis because I might break a leg, so what's with my going for a walk with a killer giraffe? Not me. From now on you take the walks with Daisy—alone."

"No. We'll leave her behind," insisted Jock gallantly, dragging me out of the back of the house.

We sneaked around the house, nipped past the vegetable garden, and tiptoed down a path where Daisy couldn't see us. For the first quarter of a mile or so we glanced back apprehensively just to make sure we hadn't been discovered. Of course we had. That damn eyesight of hers, best in the world—what had we expected? Delighted to have spotted us, she gave a little happy leap in the air as if to say, "Here I come," and with legs flying (unlike Nureyev's) she charged, flat out (giraffe have been clocked doing thirty-two miles per hour), and scared the hell out of me. Even Jock admitted to a "violent adrenaline flush."

That evening Jock telephoned Rutherfurd to see if he knew any way of avoiding getting killed by Daisy. Rutherfurd suggested that if Jock stood his ground until the last minute and then jumped aside, he would probably be O.K., because when Daisy was traveling in a straight line at high speed it would be difficult for her to change course suddenly. Jock thought this a splendid idea and calls it his "contingency plan." I thought it was a lousy idea, and quit.

Acting terribly British and believing he should never be defeated by anything—the Antarctic, the Germans, mental illness, much less a giraffe—and unable, therefore, to accept my easy "If at first you don't succeed, give up" philosophy, Jock had yet another idea so that I would change my mind and go for a walk with him and his friend. Do you know what he did? He made me a sandwich board out of burlap stuffed with kapok. It goes over my shoulders and hangs down below my knees, and I am to wear it with rubber knee boots and a motorcycle helmet—and look like some demented monster. I told him I wouldn't even go in a suit of armor.

My friend Doria suggested a noisemaker—like a New Year's Eve whirlaround, but who's going to be the first to try it to see if it

97

works? Not I, not even in my burlap outfit. Someone else suggested an instantly inflatable tree or an electric prodder—but by the time Daisy was close enough to give her the shock it would be too late. Yet another person suggested a whip, but I had the best suggestion of all: no more walks.

So every evening Daisy and Jock go on their walk, alone, with Jock racing from tree to tree and Daisy flat out after him while I just watch the Laurel and Hardy scene.

Rutherfurd stopped in, and of course he just stood there and let Daisy charge him. He was in the open when Daisy spotted him and headed right for him. I shouted, "You better watch out—she isn't used to you."

To which he replied, "Then she'd better get used to me," and just stood there in his arrogant way. Daisy ran at him and at the last minute dodged—*she* dodged, he didn't. But then maybe she remembered him from Soy and knows he's no one to mess with.

That evening we were having dinner with our old friend Michael Wood, who founded, and continues to run, the Flying Doctor Service in East Africa. I asked him about giraffe bites and he confessed that mine was the first he had encountered, though he had seen people injured or killed by giraffe kicks. Uh-huh.

If you can get him on the subject, he has bizarre tales about people being carried twelve miles impaled on elephant tusks and still surviving to talk about it. He will tell you of injuries caused by hippo tramplings, crocodile manglings, python squeezings, poisoned-arrow wounds, and a hundred other things he and his team of doctors are called upon to take care of in remote corners of the country almost every day of the week. Actually, the most common injuries, he says, involve people sleeping out of doors who are bitten by hyena, often in the face.

Most of the work of the Flying Doctors is taking medicine, preventive and otherwise, to Africans in remote areas who would receive little or no help but for the weekly flying visits of Michael's team. When necessary, quite major operations are performed by the doctors under the most rudimentary conditions.

Visitors to East Africa often become aware of Flying Doctors in another context. If a stout German has a heart attack in Serengeti or an American lady slips in the shower while staying in Tsavo National Park, they can be whisked out in no time by the Flying Doctors and taken to major hospitals in Nairobi for expert care.

Among the enthusiastic followers of our Daisy project are Betsy and Walter Cronkite, friends whom we see in New York and who came on safari here. They brought their daughter Cathy and son Chip, who was seventeen years old at the time, and on the second night, while camping in the Maasai Mara area two hundred miles from Nairobi, Chip developed severe stomach pains. Walter, who prides himself on being an amateur doctor, made a diagnosis of appendicitis. It was now eight o'clock at night and they were about thirty miles by rough track from Keekorok Lodge, the nearest point where they might find help. Piling Chip on a mattress into the back of the Land Rover, they bumped to the Lodge, and by the time they arrived there he was in a great deal of pain and it was getting worse.

Among the forty-odd tourists staying at the Lodge there was no doctor, though the Cronkites learned that they had just missed one who had left that afternoon to continue his safari in Tanzania. There is no telephone at Keekorok, only a short-wave radio, and while there are special listening-in times it is not possible to call Nairobi out of schedule. It was now about nine o'clock at night, and Walter and Betsy decided to drive to the nearest telephone at the little village of Narok, eighty miles away. If they failed to get a doctor on the line at least they would be part of the way back to Nairobi.

They trundled off into the night, still on a very bad road within the Game Park, dodging animals that appeared suddenly in their headlights and keeping a special eye open for elephant and rhino— which when dazzled by headlights can do very unpredictable things, such as turn your car over. Along the way they were stopped at two checkpoints, presumably set up to frustrate the movement of poachers' vehicles at night, and had a hard time convincing the Game Scouts and police in charge that they were not poachers but making a legitimate night movement. The men insisted on shining a torch at Chip, prodding the mattress to see if it contained poached leopard skins, and generally trying to do their job, I suppose.

At the Narok Police Station, bureaucracy was carried to a new high. The night constable told Walter that telephone calls cost the Government money, and that if he was going to accept Walter's shillings on behalf of the cashier, who didn't come back to duty until the following morning, then a lengthy form had to be completed before he could permit the use of the telephone. This is just the kind of thing one needs after driving around remote Africa all night with a son seriously ill with appendicitis. (Jock's father died of peritonitis many years ago, afflicted by it far from a hospital so that it was too late by the time he reached a doctor.)

I have to back up a minute. During the Cronkites' day and a half in Nairobi before setting out on the safari, one Carl Schlesinger, who was the P.R. man for the Flying Doctors, approached Walter for an interview. Since they are funded entirely by voluntary contributions, Schlesinger's job was to keep his eye open for V.I.P. visitors with the idea of getting publicity for the work of the Flying Doctors, which in turn would help them in their efforts to raise money. Walter, who is such a nice man, explained he would be glad to give him an interview but he simply didn't have any time in Nairobi—he was coming to us for dinner and would be off early in the morning on safari. However, he added, next time Schlesinger came to the States he would be happy to help him in any way he could. The encounter was brief and Walter forgot about it.

Now, in the Narok Police Station, Walter searched urgently for the Flying Doctors' number in the telephone book and placed the call. After a long delay the operator told him that there had been a heavy storm in Nairobi and some of the telephone lines were down and out of order, including that of the Flying Doctor Service.

Walter says that if the P.R. man's name had been Smith or Jones he would have forgotten it then and there, but the name Schlesinger had stuck with him. Thumbing through the S's in the directory, he quickly found Schlesinger and reached him at home.

While small aircraft can take off all right from Nairobi at night, there were no landing lights on the little grass strip at Narok, so the plane could not come at once, but a doctor-pilot left in the dark, timing his arrival for dawn, and picked up the whole Cronkite family, and by 8:15 A.M. Chip's appendix had been removed in Nairobi Hospital—just in time.

The rest of the Cronkite safari was spent in and around the hospital, and by the time Chip was well enough to be moved their holiday had ended. The nice part for us was that we got to see much more of them than would have been the case had they been out on safari.

A sequel to the story made us laugh. The day after the drama Jock ran into someone who works for the Flying Doctors and asked her whether she had heard about the Cronkite emergency. She said that she had indeed heard: on the morning of the rescue Carl Schlesinger, a fine P.R. man with all the right instincts for his trade, burst into the office shouting, "Something *wonderful* has happened!"

5

The Lovely One

There was a lack of pandemonium. We just happened to notice it one morning. The reason, we decided, was that Daisy was settling into a daily routine, starting with aimless breakfasting off the trees, which put her in a mood of gentle sweetness. Then there followed serene cud chewing, carrot treats every hour or so, and an afternoon nap on the lawn which gave way, as evening approached, to a vivacious strut accelerating to perilous playful runs around the garden. If she was lucky she would be taken for what Jock still insisted on describing as a walk, and finally at dusk she would be given her milk, more carrots, and put to bed.

Since this pattern was becoming regular, and since we had not been to our coast house for months, we decided to get a giraffe-sitter and go for a week. Neither of us really wanted to leave Daisy, but this was getting ridiculous—we were going to have to be away from time to time, and now was as good a moment as any to give it another try.

The journey, usually filled with enough elephant to remind us of dignity and enough baboon to make us laugh, is 378 miles east and one mile down. Along the way the long dry grass is pink and fluffy and it waves and sparkles in the sunny breeze, while Kilimanjaro—the "mountain with salt on it"—looms as a lonely backdrop. Then, descending, the landscape changes and giant baobabs stand fat and contented in their garden of dry bush, till finally, near the sea, a thousand tall palm trees look down on the lush green rug at their feet which ends abruptly at one edge, cut off by the bluest of emerald-blue seas. And there sits Mombasa island, squatting snugly with its Indian Ocean view.

Most places Jock and I have seen around the world look better in *National Geographic*, but not the eastern coast of Africa.

There aren't too many colorful cities on the globe these days, and an awful creeping uniformity works to make Teheran look like Frankfurt, and Johannesburg indistinguishable from Indianapolis, even giving London hints of New York. Yet Mombasa is unto itself, an old world which has largely been bypassed by skyscrapers and other modernization and still persists in emitting a slightly sinister Ali Baba flavor of mosques, of women in purdah, spices, and laziness; it even smells like nowhere else. Mombasa looks like an artistic stage set for a Broadway play and makes me want to clap.

Upon arrival we always drive immediately to a marvelous grundgy restaurant where we buy the best hot kebabs and cold passion fruit juice in the world. This sustains us for the last leg of our trip, seventy-eight miles north along the cost to Malindi. On this part of the journey we cross on an old ferry over what the British insist upon calling a creek, but what we smart Americans would call an inlet or a sound.

Usually the road journey is relaxing and pleasing, but this time it was terrible—a most macabre trip. The only game we saw was a dead elephant on the side of the road, and then a dead mother baboon in the middle of it, with her baby sitting on her hugging her, then tugging at her to get up. The little thing would lean down and look into his mother's eyes—can't animals recognize dead eyes? Then it would sit on her, happy for a moment searching for fleas, before tugging wildly again, beseeching her to rise, to come and play or at least give a reassuring hug once more. A little further on a dik-dik—one of the very few animals that are truly monogamous—

102

dashed in front of the car to be killed with a thud under the right front wheel, and, receding in the rearview mirror, its spouse stood piteously alone.

It started to rain heavily and we had to swerve violently once to avoid halving a ten-foot python. The favorite filthy restaurant was closed when we reached Mombasa (never open during lunch or dinner hour—only in between) and fifty minutes later the ferry broke down with us aboard and we drifted helplessly with the tide, up the creek without a paddle. When finally we were rescued and towed to safety it was late, and fatigue of the demoralizing kind enveloped us when we entered our beach house to find a scorpion in the loo and the *makuti* (palm thatch) roof leaking in the steady downpour. "It only leaks over every bed," Charo, the caretaker, told us with unconscious black humor, because really he was trying to comfort us that there were dry patches in between. We hadn't been to Malindi for nearly six months and things were in bad shape, including our rubber mattress, which had chosen to turn a sickly gray and disintegrate. Jock wanted to bury it instead of putting it outside for disposal—he was embarrassed that someone might see it.

Things did not seem much better in the light of morning either. We drove up to the village to telephone Nairobi and learned that Daisy had spent the whole of the previous day standing in her spot, waiting for us. I was so upset that when we got back to our beach house I took the yellow button which had come off my blouse the night before and was lying on my bedside table and swallowed it with a gulp of water, mistaking it for my daily vitamin pill.

For lunch Charo fried the fish in shutter oil. It was quite good, actually, so things were looking up. Charo isn't dumb—far from it—but how should he know oil for wood from oil for frying when both were in unmarked bottles? I can't tell which wild berries are edible and which will kill you—knowledge so fundamental to him that he couldn't conceive of a person not knowing it. I learned something when I first came to Africa nearly twenty years ago: people should be judged by their standards, not by yours. But still I find myself taken by surprise, unable to apply it sometimes. Once, on a trip to Nairobi, I handed Charo his picnic lunch and was intrigued to see him eat the chocolate cake before the BLT sandwich. "Does he like eating backwards or couldn't he wait for the cake?" I whispered to Jock who explained that since Charo wasn't used to eating either chocolate cake or BLT sandwiches it probably made no difference to him. (Not that Jock is in any position to comment on these

103

things. On his first trip to the States, when he stayed with my sister, he fixed himself a bowl of Gravy Train for breakfast.) However, the time Charo mixed up a salad for lunch—cold fish, hard-boiled eggs, tomatoes, lettuce, green peppers, and rice pudding—it made a difference to *me*; and since we had nothing else to eat in the house and a guest staying, I washed the whole mess under running water, thereby getting rid of the evaporated milk and the brown sugar but leaving the rice (and just a few raisins) in the salad.

Listen, Charo is smart, with a keen natural intelligence, but we went through a lot of employees before we were lucky enough to find him. One, I remember, was so dumb he called me "Bwana" for two years, and another while serving at dinner would let out these enormously loud and revolting burps right in everyone's ear. Then we had one who smoked *bhangi* (hashish) all day, and yet another who was light-fingered. They came and they went, this unfortunate succession of misfits, and one evening years later we tried to recall them all, and were able to count—and rename—seven: Stealy, Smelly, Burpy, Dummy, Drunky, Hashful and Clot.

Malindi, a charming old fishing village on the edge of a large bay, used to be an Arab sultanate and slave-trading post. The dhows still sail as they did in Biblical times and the fishermen still fish in their fetchingly traditional ways. The monsoons and the mangoes are still the same—in fact, nothing much has changed other than the addition of a few hotels along the bay and the opening of the Mickey Mouse Fashion House, where you can buy clothes ready-made from African fabrics. If you want clothes tailored specially there is a brothel nearby where the girls "sunlight" as couturières.

Ten years ago Jock and I built a Zanzibar-type house a mile or two south of Malindi. It has open areas and wooden doors and shutters, and it stands almost in the Indian Ocean. We spend much time there writing. Japanese publishers, we are told, lock their writers in hotel rooms, and Jock and I do the same thing to ourselves by going to Malindi. We have no telephone, and the quiet and the beautiful visual aids of sea and tranquil white sand are more conducive perhaps than a Nagoya motel to uninterrupted hours at the typewriter.

Thus I was surprised on about the third morning to hear an extraordinary loud noise like a cross between a foghorn being strangled and a giant's burp. "What's that?" I called somewhat alarmed to Jock.

"A camel," he answered knowingly. Sure enough, there it was, standing in the sand right in front of our house with its Somali owner, who had driven it, evidently, from the Northern Province to go into the business of taking the German and American tourists for a ride—both financially and literally. As the camel left I noticed some of its droppings, so I got a plastic bag, dropped some droppings into it, and mailed them to a friend of mine in Philadelphia who hadn't written enough to please me. It worked: I had a letter back in no time thanking me for the camel dung and saying that it would make her Nativity scene more realistic, come Christmas.

Camels are so romantic, but this time, instead of enchanting me with visions of empty deserts and lights flickering in the sky and in Bedouin Paul Newman's tent, I thought of Daisy.

Giraffe and camels aren't supposed to be related but they look alike to me, particularly their mouths and the shape of their heads, and they both have long necks, and come from the same part of the world. They seem like cousins, certainly more than a giraffe and an okapi which is supposed to be the giraffe's closest relative. (The okapi is a dopey-looking antelope with black and white stripes around its legs which make it look like a cow that got mixed up with a zebra.) Then there is a thing called the inguinal fold which extends from the hind leg to the belly in other ungulates (hoofed animals), but neither the camel nor the giraffe has it. How's that for research? But I read, in those books about giraffe which tell all about the inguinal folds and blah blah blah, that a camel and a giraffe are *not* related. I do not believe it.

Another reason I don't believe it is that a giraffe and a camel are the only two animals in the world who walk by moving both legs on the same side forward at the same time. (All other quadrupeds have a form of diagonal gait.) Horses can be trained to do this same-sided arrangement when trotting, and they are taught to move this way especially for harness racing. Giraffe and *their relations* the camels never trot, though; they either walk or canter or gallop.

People cannot be expected to know everything—except we Americans, who feel that not only should we *know* everything but we should be *better* at everything, too. That's why I think I have to know all about giraffe. (In contrast to this attitude I have a British friend who thought cholesterol was a card game until two weeks ago when we told him, and he wasn't even ashamed.)

So I took notes from all the books I read on giraffe and marked what I found interesting and left out the Latin names of the five kinds of ticks they get, so if that is what turns you on you'll have to

105

get the books yourself. But if not, here goes with some of the abstruse and intriguing things about giraffe—with our comments added, now that we know more about them than the scientists do. For example, one zoologist writes, "Their tongues are fairly rough, greyish in color, slim and pointed, and 16″ long." But how many of these zoologists have ever kissed a wild giraffe and felt its tongue? I want you to know that a giraffe's tongue is fairly smooth, is a pretty dark-purplish color, and looks and acts like a nice snake: it can sit up, curl around and up and down and, reminiscent of an elephant's trunk, can coil around branches, dodging thorns, or into my mouth looking for carrots, and up the giraffe's own nose. It is also seventeen inches long.

I exaggerate, and when Jock chastises me for it I reply that when I'm telling a story I don't want to be bothered with the facts. But C. A. W. Guggisberg, the well-known zoologist, says a giraffe's tongue is seventeen inches long, too.

I don't care if they have thirty-two teeth or not, do you? But I do think it's fascinating that a giraffe has the same amount of neck vertebrae as a mouse—and practically all of us other mammals too.

Bragging, I also already told you giraffe have the largest brain of all the hoofed animals, but I'd like to tell you again. It is a fact, but without a specially devised I.Q. test to compare giraffe to sheep and impala and horses and dik-dik and about a hundred other hoofed animals (can you imagine arranging such a test?), it is hard to be definite about comparative intelligence. Jock, who has had a lot of experience down on the farm and who can milk a cow and shear a sheep and all such things, says he would guess that at six months Daisy is a good deal more switched on (British always say that) than a six-month-old calf or a foal. When she was stuck in the fishpond, for instance, he said he could actually watch a calculated mental process under way: following a logical assessment of what had to be done, Daisy put her plan into action and extricated herself. (Personally I thought she was stupid for going in in the first place, but he assures me that a cow stuck in a bog just flounders around and exhausts itself.)

Daisy also seems to get the message pretty fast, whatever the message may be, and adapts to routines after only a few times. She has a mind of her own and will not be bullied or conned into doing anything she doesn't want to do. (Another chief; still no Indians in our family.) We may think it is time for her to be put back into her boma so that we can go to the early movie, but if she doesn't feel like it there is no way we will get her in. Equally, when we want to show her off to our friends by getting her to kiss us or to go for a short walk she will cooperate only if it pleases her—which is probably the sure sign of having a large brain and being extremely smart.

Most authorities will tell you giraffe make no sound, but we'll blow that theory later on. They may also tell you that they have curling eyelashes, but in point of fact the lashes are very straight.

And you may hear, too, that giraffe don't graze and usually chew their cud standing up. Daisy usually chews her cud sitting down, and she even grazes sitting down—stretching her neck to eat the grass around her—like a Roman empress. Which brings us to giraffe sitting or lying down:

One day, trying to impress Rutherfurd, I said to him, "Want to see me walk up to Daisy while she's sitting down?"

Rutherfurd said flatly, "Giraffe don't sit down."

"Whaddaya mean they don't sit down?" I shouted, pointing at Daisy.

Of course he didn't answer; he doesn't say anything twice.

"Jock," I yelled, pointing to Daisy sitting on the lawn, "Rutherfurd says giraffe don't sit down."

"They don't," agreed Jock, coolly regarding Daisy.

"I want my mother," I whined.

But Jock did come to my rescue. "They *lie* down. Horses or cows do not sit, either."

"What does Shirley Brown do?" I asked.

"She lies *and* sits."

I said, "To me, lying has got to be with your head flat. Daisy doesn't do that."

"To me, sitting has to be with hindquarters down, front legs straight. Daisy doesn't do that."

Stalemate.

Nobody will ever be able to convince me that Daisy Rothschild, that sensitive, delicate, gentle girl-creature, is thick-skinned, but a rude scientist says, ". . . the hide is at least one inch thick and very tough."

Their patterns are their fingerprints; no two giraffe are marked alike, so Daisy's butterflies will identify her easily and forever. Jock and I could tell Daisy from any other giraffe, but the only way we could prove it to a third person would be by having a photograph or accurate sketch of her particular butterflies. As far as we know this is

107

the only way of telling giraffe apart, unless of course through something obvious like one of them having a scar or being an albino or something. As a matter of fact there *is* an albino giraffe running with a herd near the Mara, and for years Jock and I have looked for it. A safari client, who had made only one trip here, was showing us his slides one evening back in Chicago and said very casually, "See the all-white giraffe in that herd?" He didn't realize he may have one of the very few pictures in existence of that albino. Does the poor thing know it's an albino? Without a mirror how could he tell, unless all his friends say, "Hey, you dumb albino . . ."

Everyone who has observed giraffe for any length of time will mention with delight how they have seen them "do this thing with their necks." Swinging their necks, they deliver a looping sideways blow, usually to the neck of another giraffe. It is mainly the males who do this, but Rutherfurd has seen a male and a female engaged in the "game." It is quite a spectacle, and Guggisberg describes it as "a titanic slugging match . . . with movements of the battling giants by no means devoid of a certain monumental grace . . . with their necks swaying like masts . . ." Some people call it "necking," but the scientists tell us it is fighting and maybe they are right. I wonder, though, if they are really fighting, why wouldn't they use their fearsome kicks as well? And why would they fight? They are not territorial animals and it doesn't seem to be over girls as far as anyone can tell. I prefer to think of it as a sport they enjoy, like two boxers going into a ring to spar. Who knows?

Professor B. Grzimek once came across a dead giraffe literally hanging from a tree in Serengeti National Park. He wrote, "Whilst browsing close to a river the animal had slipped on the bank, lost its footing and its head had become inextricably wedged in the fork of a tree." I mean how does he know it didn't commit suicide?

Another thing I learned from Dr. Guggisberg is that the main defense of the giraffe is not its kick, lethal though that may be in extremis, but the simple fact of being very alert and therefore seldom finding itself in troublesome situations. Jock and I have been so impressed by Daisy that we are thinking of giving her a uniform and hiring her as a watch giraffe. We can be talking to her or giving her her carrot fix when suddenly she will stare intently in one direction and her ears will jerk forward. We have learned that it is *never* a false alarm, though the movement that has triggered it may be as simple as Shem opening the kitchen window a hundred yards away or the owl family which live in the roof of our sunroom taking off on their evening foray. Jock said that, quite seriously, were he in the Kenya Army he would consider using a giraffe as a sentry, because nothing, but *nothing*, can move within their incredibly wide field of vision without attracting their immediate attention. Can't you just picture Daisy saluting in a tall black fuzzy hat like the one Jock used to wear on guard at Buckingham Palace? Daisy does not give the impression of being constantly on the lookout, and in fact she sometimes appears to be lackadaisycal (bad pun) or wholly engrossed in a particularly succulent-looking acacia branch, but the reflex must be so inbuilt that even in a relaxed state she is still one hundred percent alert visually. Not only is giraffe's eyesight fantastically good, but many scientists believe that their color perception is far superior to a human's.

When archaeologists first started to decipher the hieroglyphics in Egyptian ruins they found that one of the recurring symbols was a giraffe, and by the time they broke the code, so to speak, it was apparent that "giraffe" meant foretell or predict. Having been around Daisy for some months I can vouch that those Egyptians were pretty smart, because Daisy knows before Shirley Brown, or the horses, or the bushbuck, or the guinea fowl, or any of the other animals to be found around our property, when something or someone is approaching.

Guggisberg claims that many giraffe *are* killed by lion, but only when the cats hunt in packs or take them by surprise. If the giraffe sees the sneaky lion in time the King of the Beasts usually ends up getting the worst of the encounter. Other enemies include leopard, which we have mentioned, and crocodile, which have grabbed many a giraffe while they are in their vulnerable drinking position at the water's edge. Wild dog and hyena are also a menace for young giraffe. To protect her young from attack a mother will often put her baby under her stomach so that it won't accidentally be the recipient of one of her own deadly kicks.

The Roman poet Horace named the giraffe the "camelopard," and it was so known for hundreds of years. Well, I for one know where he got the camel part from, but *leopard?* A spotted camel? It's a pretty dumb description, but you've got to consider that that was thousands of years ago. But wait till you hear this: Dr. Samuel Johnson in his dictionary published as recently as 1755 defines the giraffe as simply being "taller than an elephant, but not so thick." No comment.

It wasn't until the 1500s that some Swiss naturalist even ques-

109

tioned the ramifications of a cross between a camel and a leopard and stated categorically that it could not possibly be true. And finally, in 1543, Pierre Belon, another of the early naturalists, called the giraffe *zarafah*—an Arabic word meaning "the lovely one."

Greek successors of the Pharaohs, the Ptolemies, were famous for the menageries they kept in Alexandria, and records show that Ptolemy II was the owner of a giraffe. In 46 B.C. Julius Caesar brought one from Egypt to Rome which may well have been a present from Cleopatra. One of the earliest recorded items in Kenya is the fact that in 1414 a giraffe was sent from Malindi to a Chinese emperor. When the *tsu-la* was received in the Great Hall of Receptions by Emperor Yung Lo it created a sensation, and it became the emblem in China of perfect peace, perfect harmony, and perfect virtue and was treated as sacred. Little wonder, if anything like Daisy.

The first camelopard set foot on American soil in 1837 and headed for a zoo.

Every explorer, Livingstone included, wrote at length about them, and Theodore Roosevelt managed to walk within ten feet of a reticulated giraffe which was standing dozing under a thorn tree. The animal suddenly awoke, then reared up and chopped at him with a left forefoot, but the blow un/fortunately (depending on your view of history) fell short.

For millions of years giraffe lived in Africa on savannas which have since turned into deserts, and the lovely ones vanished there along with the vegetation. They were shot at way before the white man appeared. Guggisberg tells us that the rock paintings and engravings of the Sahara of thousands of years ago depict giraffe being shot with bows and arrows and trapped by means of snares of exactly the type that are still in use in Africa today. They consist of a wooden circle with sharp spokes pointing inward, overlapping each other in the center. This contraption, tied to a heavy log with a long rope, is placed over a hole in the ground and camouflaged with sand or earth. A giraffe putting its foot through the springy wooden spokes has no possibility of escaping and finds itself helplessly anchored by the leg.

Elsewhere giraffe were stalked on foot and attacked by men with spears and poisoned arrows. In many places they were killed not only for their meat and their hides, which make excellent buckets and water bottles, but also for their tails, to which certain tribes attributed magical properties, and which others used as badges of office for their chiefs and kings. The long black hairs of the tail were

110

prized—and still are. Not long ago Jock and I saw a giraffe lying dead in the bush, poached just for the tail hairs so that someone could make a bracelet to sell for perhaps five shillings (seventy-five cents). People should not buy giraffe-hair bracelets, of course, but if the thing is in a shop they understandbly assume there is no harm to it—they just don't think about how it comes to be for sale. If ever they saw a beautiful giraffe dead from a poacher's poisoned arrow they'd never buy another.

The excellent Guggisberg also states: "No camelopard seems to have been willfully killed in Rome until about AD 180 when Commodus, son of the great Marcus Aurelius, slaughtered one in the arena." Never mind, we white folk have been busy making up for lost time.

The white farmers in South Africa massacred as many as they could because they found that giraffe hides far surpassed those of other animals for making strong thongs for harnessing the trek oxen and making long whips. African hunters, armed and equipped by white traders, slaughtered all the giraffe in the Kalahari, where Livingstone and others had encountered and written wondrous things about them. The slaughter of giraffe increased a hundredfold with the introduction of firearms, and between the two World Wars the giraffe were butchered at an unprecedented rate.

Shortly after the turn of the century Schillings wrote, "The day cannot be far when the last *twiga* will close its beautiful eyes." Wouldn't you think that since he wrote that we would have done something more about conserving not only giraffe but all the game, now that we know, now that we're aware? The answer, sadly, is no. Even those who should be enlightened often aren't. I refer just as an example to a Nairobi couple I know (I shall no longer call them friends) who have placed a huge giraffe skin on their living-room floor and are "decorating their whole room around it." They are very proud of it—they shot it themselves. Forty-one licenses were issued last year to shoot giraffe.

Why? What kind of a person can shoot a giraffe? It can't be for sport, because giraffe just stand there and look at you through those long eyelashes. How could anyone pull the trigger? For a rug?

If they want to hunt giraffe as the Hamran Arabs of the Sudan and the Boran in northern Kenya did, on horseback, galloping up close to hamstring them with their long straight swords—that at least is a sport and even then was considered "the most thrilling adventure."

111

Sir Samuel Baker reported that whenever the Arabs of the Sudan offered him a horse they declared it could "overtake a giraffe"—there was no higher recommendation. Long ago in Arabia if a horse could do this twice in a day it was declared to be "fit for a king." Others in the Sudan chased giraffe in parties of five or six riders and killed their quarry with lances. Baker says:

> This was not accomplished without a certain amount of danger and accidents were fairly frequent. Successful giraffe hunters were therefore greatly respected and the memory of their deeds went down in local history.
>
> One Sheikh became famous for having speared twenty-five, while another was remembered as the man who killed fifteen from the back of one and the same horse.

Sheikh Rutherfurd? On Douglas? He doesn't kill them, though; he saves them.

Would you like a little Rutherfurd history now? More than what a person does, I am intrigued by what makes him do it, what motivates him, so I asked Rutherfurd to tell me about himself. It was a total waste of time and I should have saved my breath, for, being typically British, he feels uncomfortable talking about himself, has been taught that modesty is golden, and considered my direct questions very bad form. But, full of bad form, I dug right in:

"Where were you born?"

"Nakuru."

"Did your mother and father live in Kenya long before you were born?"

"Yes."

"Were they born in Kenya?" I asked eagerly, because third-generation European families here mean history. "Did your grandmother live in Kenya, too?"

"Yes." Nothing more.

"You'd be great on a talk show."

"I beg your pardon?"

"How did they get here?"

After hours, days actually, of doing a sneak interview, I finally pieced his story together: In 1910 his grandmother arrived in Kenya all alone from Scotland. Her son was already ensconced in Sandhurst (Britain's West Point) and she left her husband, whom she decided she didn't like—bully for her, especially in those days—and was among the first women to smoke, and to ride astride, and the first, perhaps the only, professional hunter of her sex here. I have certainly never heard of another woman taking out a hunting party. During World War I, when the British fought the Germans for possession of German East Africa, later named Tanganyika and later still Tanzania, Grandmother Rutherfurd drove an oxcart with a huge red cross on it and nursed the wounded British soldiers. One old man still claims that if it weren't for her taking a bullet out of his stomach he wouldn't be alive today. Another friend tells how she shot a lion off the top of him and thereby saved his life.

(Where are the people like that now? Then we had Ewart Grogan, who walked from Cape Town to Cairo for a girl, and Lord Delamare, who pioneered ranching against awful odds, we had Isak Dinesen—the ranks of adventuresome spirits were filled. I guess the world is too civilized and too small now to allow us to be brave explorers, intrepid pioneers.)

After the war, all alone, Grandma Rutherfurd bought a three-thousand-acre farm near Nakuru (a hundred miles west of Nairobi) because it had more game on it than any land she had ever seen, and she stocked it with cattle and settled down to a life of happily ever after. Her son fought in World War I in France and arrived in Kenya in 1925, met a girl from Ireland and married her in 1927. John Andrew Rutherfurd was born to them in 1928 (September 20, all you astrology jocks out there), the oldest of three children—all eleven months apart. They lived near Grandmother Rutherfurd's farm and he said he "toted a rifle before I was as tall as one." Riding and shooting were as much a part of his life as hopscotch and roller skating were a part of mine.

I asked him if he had friends close by and he answered, "Our neighbor's sons were the two closest friends my brother and I had. We used to walk over and play with them frequently."

"How far away were they?"

"About thirty miles."

Can't you hear it: "Hey, Mom, I'm going next door to play with Tony—be back next week."

Like Jock and others who grew up in remote places in the Kenya of those days, he didn't go to school until he was eight years old, but a tutor lived at home to teach the children to read and write "whenever she could catch us." Then off to boarding school at Gilgil, where he and Jock overlapped, and where McDonnell, my younger son, enrolled twenty years later.

When Rutherfurd was seventeen years old he went to England and "joined the K.O.S.B."

"What's that?" I asked, thinking, KOSB—a radio station?

"Jock would know."

"Do I have to call up Jock and ask him? Can't you tell me?"

"King's Own Scottish Borderers."

I made no comment at what I thought was a very odd name but merely nodded and asked him how many years he was in the K.O.S.B.

"Four," was the monosyllablic answer.

"Were you commissioned?"

"I've been commissioned three times."

"*Three* times?"

"Yes."

"Isn't that rather unusual?" I asked this unusual man. "Why three times?"

Exasperated, he nevertheless laughed and his nose wrinkled up. He may be quiet but he is never in the least unpleasant, and so with a sigh and a swig of his usual warm White Cap beer he surrendered and told me that he was a "leftenant" when he came out of the K.O.S.B.; that he went back to Kenya, joined the Kenya Regiment to fight in the Mau Mau emergency, and came out a captain; and that he joined the Kenya Regiment again as a Territorial (National Guard) and came out a major.

"Did you have no desire to stay in England?"

"I farmed there awhile, but I wanted to get back to Kenya."

After a lot more probing and cajoling and a few more White Caps he told me an amusing story: He was in the Army in Germany in 1951 when his duty was up, so he bought a "Peep"—Dodge's military version of a power wagon—for £200. (He was also disgusted that I had never even heard of a Peep. After all, I was an American, wasn't I?) He and a Kenya-born Danish friend planned to drive from London to Nairobi. They each had £150 and figured it would cost at least that, so what they decided they needed was another £150 for fun and games (my words, not his) and they advertised in the London *Telegraph* for someone to join them on their mad adventure. Many people answered, but everyone wanted a free ride. Finally one Christopher Deverell, an Etonian, appeared in answer to the ad, and although he had had no experience bashing around Africa (and according to Rutherfurd "probably had never fired a gun except in a twenty-one-gun salute in Hyde Park") he was the only one to answer who had £150. Deverell was in the King's Troop, R.H.A.,

114

said Rutherfurd, just as if I knew what he was talking about (Jock told me later R.H.A. is Royal Horse Artillery), and had been posted to East Africa as a gunner, but the military seemed to be having some difficulty getting him there—he had missed the troopship or something—and he convinced them that this would be as good a way as any.

Rutherfurd and his buddy took Deverell's money, and despite the lack of a guarantee that they'd get him any further than Dover he set off with them. First stop Paris, where to the disgruntled astonishment of the two Kenya cowboys Deverell joined his mother in an elegant hotel. The other two tore up Paris.

In Spain they bought sherry in jerry-cans, and in Gibraltar the Navy put them on the ferry for Tangiers. Their Peep was so loaded with equipment and supplies for their one-month trip (which turned out to be three months) that the only way to get it on the ferry was to have it hoisted aboard by the Navy's crane. Thanking the Navy very much, they sailed to Tangiers, but when they got there they couldn't get the Peep *off* the ferry and there was no Navy to rescue them. The skipper of the ferry, who was "laughing his bloody head off," said he would try to unload the car with his equipment, inadequate as it was, but made them sign a paper saying that if he dropped it into the drink it wasn't his fault. They signed, and the skipper and his inefficient gear succeeded in unloading them in exotic Tangiers.

No guns were allowed in Tangiers at that time, and the Three Musketeers were carrying an arsenal. They bribed the customs man with a carton of Players cigarettes to keep the guns hidden, but when they returned the next day they learned they had all been confiscated. It took them a long time to hunt down the British consul, who listened to the story aghast, picked up a telephone and spoke in three languages, then told them to go to a certain police station to collect their guns and to get the hell out of there and not come back. Ever.

The coast road to Algiers (then French) was lovely, Rutherfurd said. Along the way they decided that in case of an emergency, which seemed to occur every fifteen minutes, they should have something tangible to help them, so they got Deverell into a pair of clean pants and sent him to the French commandant to get written permission to proceed and a flag to wave—the NATO Pact flag. Deverell obtained the letter, which none of them could read. They hoped it would work.

There were two routes across the Sahara, and of course they

picked the impossible one. The Government told them that the way to go was not alone—that they had to travel with an army convoy or pay £50 each (enough, I guess, to cover the cost of burying the bodies and sending cables to distraught families), but if a miracle occurred and they *did* make it, they could get their £50 back in Nairobi, which later they did. (Two miracles, I figure.)

For the Sahara crossing they had fitted three extra gas tanks on the Peep and they had filled up with petrol where it was cheaper, but with the weight of the extra cans and the rough going the Peep's springs broke. As they were sitting in the sand looking forlorn the Foreign Legion came by and they showed them the letter. They were saluted immediately, taken to the Legion camp, ushered into the officers' mess and served a seven-course meal with several wines, which they drank leisurely while a Legionnaire spent the rest of the day fixing the springs. Deverell wasn't so bad after all.

After many lonely days of traversing the desert they spotted something moving in the south. It was the first thing other than a camel that they had seen for hundreds of miles, and as it approached they could make out that it was a Land Rover and grew very excited. A bearded man alighted from it, waved, and called, *"Bonjour."* Since Deverell's French was supposedly better than the other two's, he went over to ask how the roads were to the south. Deverell was not getting very far with the bearded man's French—until he discovered that he too was English, and that they had been to Eton together. Can't you just see those two Etonians standing in the middle of the desert painfully trying to make each other understand in schoolboy French? And so it went—Rutherfurd's trip, and his life. . . .

Deverell stopped one of the first Mau Mau bullets and was invalided back to England. Rutherfurd continued fighting, and among the men of his company was an enormous African, a promising Ugandan corporal named Idi Amin—Big Daddy himself. Later Amin, the self-imposed dictator of Uganda, became tired of being a corporal or a sergeant and promoted himself to four-star general, then field marshal, and finally decreed that he would be President for life.

After the emergency was over Rutherfurd did a spell as a game warden, then turned to farming and breeding horses—and became interested in the Rothschild giraffe.

And now a little Rothschild history? In his book *Giraffe*, published in 1969, the scholarly Guggisberg, who has looked into these things very carefully, tells us that there are eight different species of giraffe remaining in Africa (there used to be thirteen, but five have already been wiped out during the last fifty years) and that of these "only 200 Rothschild remain," most of them on the Craigs' farm. Both Rutherfurd and the Craigs have taken their share in preserving these last surviving Rothschild in Kenya.

The ranch originally belonged to Delia Craig's father, Alexander Douglas—after whom Rutherfurd's horse was named. (As this story proceeds I will refer to him as A. Douglas to avoid confusion with the horse.) Delia lent us a file of correspondence about the Rothschild between her father and the Game Department dating back to 1946, with letters from neighboring farmers as well. Looking through it, we learned not only about the giraffe but about characters of thirty years ago and attitudes prevalent in Colonial Kenya.

It is clear that but for A. Douglas and the cooperation of a very sympathetic Game Department, the Rothschild species would have vanished twenty years ago. The trouble was that the areas where the giraffe lived were scheduled for agriculture, while other parts of the country had been set aside for game. Thus the Rothschilds found themselves marooned, unwanted squatters amid serious farmers. By 1946 the game warden for the area, an amazing old martinet named Colonel Swinton-Home, estimated in an official letter to the Chief Game Warden in Nairobi that there were about 850 of the giraffe altogether, with the largest single concentration on Douglas' place. The two Government officials, one in Nairobi and one in the field, wrote back and forth (sending copies of their correspondence to A. Douglas, fortunately for posterity), as they struggled to find a solution. The trouble was that the law stated clearly that a farmer was legally entitled to shoot any animal if it was doing damage to his crops or property, and one of the letters shows that the farmers were even seeking to have the giraffe classified as vermin. (Daisy— vermin!?) Unfortunately there was no provision in Government budgets for compensating farmers for damage caused by wild animals, so the only way to placate them was for Government to help eradicate the nuisance or to allow the farmers to cope with the offending animals themselves. As Swinton-Home wrote, " . . . it gives them licence to blot at sight." Obscure and confusing Government regulations were issued on the subject, and even the Chief Game Warden lamented to A. Douglas, ". . . the latest circular needs an interpreter." (Nothing ever changes.)

There was a plan to ask the farmers to cooperate in a massive drive, with horses and cars and trucks, to herd the giraffe to a designated game area thirty miles away, but it was abandoned because no one thought it could really succeed. At best they reckoned that little groups of giraffe would keep breaking back through the cordon and that most would have returned to their home territory within a week or two of being forced into the new area.

The letters cover a multitude of other subjects as well as the giraffe, and Swinton-Home is revealed as being permanently preoccupied with the inefficiency and laziness of the handful of African Game Scouts allocated to him. In a letter that reads like an extract from a script for a propaganda movie that might be made by oppressed South African blacks, he wrote to the Chief Game Warden:

> The snag is, everyone has his own idea of handling Africans, some are d—d soft with them, others d—d stiff—I am possibly amongst the latter class.
> Knowing my Black brother in South Africa and East Africa for 50 years, I can not implicitly trust any—even the best boy here I caught out selling buck [antelope] meat—he had hell from me. My advice is pay for quality and let go all the stiffs—I fear there may be many who must go . . .

A few farmers, the foremost of whom was A. Douglas, wanted to keep the giraffe, offering them some protection, but most wished the area rid of them because of damage to crops, and Swinton-Home, even though he represented Government, found his hands tied by the law when he tried to be overprotective.

There were farmers who showed their scorn in their communications with the Game Department. Since the wildlife technically belonged to the Crown (meaning His Majesty King George VI), if a farmer shot an animal larger than an antelope he was supposed to report to his local game warden. One person who had shot a giraffe on his land wrote: "I gather you require the skin and some etceteras. In that case I suggest you collect same as I am in no position to waste time carting giraffe remains around the countryside."

Another farmer, an Afrikaner called Van de Merwe, was suspected of excessive shooting even when his crops were not being damaged, and the Duke of Manchester, a great Rothschild supporter who still lives in the area, wrote to Swinton-Home: "Incidentally, I hear that Van de Merwe has been shooting them and selling the meat!!!"

On the file there are two or three of Van de Merwe's letters (if you'll forgive the expression). One, written in 1956, evidently in response to some Government questionnaire, reads thus:

DEAR SIR,
Herewith I am senting the gide to tell you about the Uganda Caps [he meant Uganda Kob, a species of antelope] they are most on my farm but they jump over the wrier as ease as pat. I am very busy with my plonting now, I already plont hundred and fifty acre of Maize. Myslerf are thinking they must be shoot at once, please. Here are plent of them and I wood like if you could come and see yourself. I don't know if they are on Mr. Basel farm because I don't go there at al. Your gide could tell you better. If you could send me some .22 shoots,* please, with your gide.

Yours faithfully,
VAN DE MERWE

Underneath there is a comment scribbled hastily by an irate Swinton-Home:

Utterly hopeless! Man can't read English or begin to understand the 7 Clear Questions put to him—and doesn't even give his address.

Poor old Swinton-Home, trapped between recalcitrant Boer farmers, uninterpretable Government circulars and lazy Game Scouts. In yet another letter to the Chief Game Warden he writes,

It is drunkenness that gets me furious IN DAY TIME. If at night, and they are sober in the morning, I pay no heed. And they get lazier and lazier unless CURSED almost daily. I frankly feel their rise of pay should not exceed Sh.10/-[$1.50] per month—or better Shs.5/- [75 cents; the average pay was just over 100 shillings ($15) per month]. I control them as much as I am able now that the KIBOKO [whip] is abolished. At my great age, rising 82, I regret that even if asked I don't feel able to undertake . . .

But despite all the difficulties and annoyances and old age, in 1956 Swinton-Home finally brought about "the Douglas solution."
A. Douglas, though often attracting the ire of his neighbors, was more than willing to be host and to provide sanctuary to the giraffe

---

*Presumably a request for ammunition from Swinton-Home with which further to decimate the animal population!

because he loved them. He did not care that they knocked down his fences—he could always put those up again—and if they caused damage on his place it was worth it for the joy of having them. Someone Up There must have been keeping an eye on the Rothschilds, because, by chance, the greatest concentration of them happened to be on A. Douglas' ranch where they were cherished.

Swinton-Home too, for all his outdated attitudes and irascibility, was the man who finally persuaded his superiors in the Game Department to make an exception in the case of A. Douglas, allowing him to buy the giraffe on his farm for the token figure of ten shillings ($1.75) per head. This gave him complete control over them, thus insulating them from pressures that other farmers might have brought to bear through the Government, though it did make him liable in law to compensate his neighbors for damage caused by "his" giraffe.

If it were not for these two men there would be no Rothschild giraffe today—and that means there would be no Daisy.

Even after A. Douglas' death, luck still followed the Rothschild. Now they belonged to Delia and David Craig, who were just as anxious to keep them alive. And whom did the Craigs get to manage the ranch? Rutherfurd.

During his tenure he kept a watchful eye over the giraffe and, as I mentioned earlier, experimented with moving some to other places, including the estate of their old friend the Duke of Manchester. But the Duke now has only five—not enough to keep the species going—and ultimately his ranch too may be taken over for peasant agriculture.

In the mid-1960s about forty Rothschild still lived on a farm east of Mount Elgon belonging to a Colonel McCall, and there were others in adjacent spots, wandering about being destructive. McCall, like A. Douglas, was a dedicated Rothschild fan, and with the help of the Government District Commissioner, David Shireff, and Rutherfurd, he decided to attempt what Swinton-Home had thought about years earlier: they would drive the giraffe to an uninhabited wild area nearby where they would be safe.

They mounted a full-scale cavalry expedition, calling in polo players who came wearing old sweaters and their helmets, show jumpers in tweed jackets, amateur jockeys on retired racehorses, farmers riding hacks, and, through the good offices of Shireff, a contingent of immaculately uniformed African Tribal Police from the Northern Province, mounted on speedy and surefooted Somali ponies. For two days this amazing troop wheeled and charged and outflanked the bewildered giraffe, finally driving them down a steep escarpment to the safety of their new home, but not before a few of the polo players and show jumpers had sustained broken collarbones and cracked ribs as they came unstuck while galloping over the rough, rock-strewn terrain. The thoroughbreds were in trouble all the time, but the Somali ponies, born to that kind of country, never so much as stumbled. Finally the intrepid horsemen limped back to base, their extraordinary mission completed. By the next morning every single giraffe, plus a few more who had joined them from below, had clambered back up the escarpment and were feeding happily right where the whole business had started. Alas, the *twigas* should have paid attention to what their saviors were trying to do for them. The McCall farm was taken over for a settlement scheme, and not one member of that herd remains alive today.

But Rutherfurd was able to keep the numbers about static at Soy. Occasionally one or two giraffe would be poached, or shot perhaps if they wandered off the Craig property, and at least five met grisly ends by being hit by a train which puffed along one edge of the ranch twice a day.

Now the poor things face their most serious crisis yet. As we said, the eighteen-thousand-acre ranch is being broken up and sold to hundreds of small farmers. The Kenya Government knew that something would have to be done and undertook an ecological survey of Lake Nakuru National Park a hundred miles away to determine if there was enough of the right kind of food there for a herd of giraffe. It is an idyllic spot and the great advantage is that no other giraffe live there, so the Rothschild characteristics will not be diluted by the infusion of different blood. The problem, as always, has been finding the money to capture and move a breeding nucleus of about twenty-five young giraffe from Soy to Nakuru.

The Craigs, Rutherfurd, Jock and I, and many others have devoted much effort to this difficult and time-consuming undertaking. You can't just round up the requisite number like cattle, load them in a truck and scoot down the road. They are wild and they are huge. Each one must be caught, soothed and fed for a while, individually crated, winched onto a truck and then held in a boma in Nakuru Park until all of them have arrived and they can be released en masse. Just to let them go one by one upon arrival would greatly diminish the chances of their re-forming into a herd.

We gave a "Giraffe Ball" at our house and were astonished at the

121

support and generosity of people. We raised enough money to save a few giraffe at least. Our good friend Harry Meyerhoff from Baltimore gave us $1,000 and offered to back a loan for more because of the urgency. (Now Daisy's name is Daisy Meyerhoff Rothschild.) We have been in touch with professional animal trappers, with the game warden at Nakuru, with officials in the Ministry of Tourism and Wildlife in Nairobi, with vets working in the Game Department, and we have tried to keep everyone in touch with everyone else. The Government posted an extra couple of Game Scouts at Soy to protect the giraffe from poachers and at the same time readied themselves at Nakuru Park, where a special fence has been built with money provided by the World Wildlife Fund to keep the giraffe out of adjacent agricultural areas. They have also looked into the practicability of moving some to another small but suitable park near Lake Victoria—but again the lack of finance is the main difficulty.

We will not know the outcome until after this book is published, but of one thing we are certain. Those giraffe which remain at Lewa Downs will not survive.

I must admit that Guggisberg did comfort me by saying that giraffe are not very territorial, because now I know that those which are moved to Nakuru will not mind the fact that they are no longer at Lewa Downs.

Also comforting, in the light of taking Daisy from her family, is the fact that he points out that their hierarchy is not as defined as in many other species, they seem to follow no hard rules, and their herds are "unstable and haphazard." He continues:

> Many observers consider a giraffe's maternal instincts are not very highly developed and the ties between mother and offspring are alleged to be fairly tenuous . . . It cannot be denied that a young giraffe frequently wanders around far from its mother, which a rhinoceros calf would never do. . . . A giraffe calf . . . is able to remain in visual contact with its mother over a considerable distance and receive optical signals from her. If it has a tendency to stray, this does not necessarily have grave consequences, and the youngster's independence need not indicate any lack of interest on the part of the mother.
>
> A striking feature of the giraffe's social behaviour are the "nurseries," groups of calves not more than a couple of months old, which are quite obviously under the care of one or two adult ani-

mals. These generally consist of about five or six youngsters but on one occasion, in the Mara Reserve, I counted a dozen calves together. The fact that giraffe mothers "hand over" their children to a "kindergarten" might perhaps be considered as an argument against parental devotion . . . I am convinced that these nurseries form and break up as casually as all other giraffe groupings. The calves are still being suckled and therefore dependent on their mothers; they are simply being looked after while most of the females have wandered off in the seemingly aimless manner so characteristic of the species.

Another report I read by a scientist stated that if the herd separates, as they frequently do, the babies by choice often go temporarily with someone else other than the mother.

This I found really cheering for a number of reasons. One, we don't have to feel too terrible about taking Daisy from her mother, not only because she'd be dead now anyway but because being with her mother is not a strong instinct and she might even have chosen not to be with her. Also, it *is* nice to feel we don't have to be with Daisy every second of the day. I never realized how much time raising Daisy Rothschild would take—certainly more than I had to devote to any of my other three children. It isn't the making of the formula and the sterilizing of the pan and the feeding four times a day that are the time-consuming part—it's having to be with her so that she won't feel lonely. Now at least I know that if she can see me it will be O.K. Every half hour or so I go to the window and call (feeling silly), "Hello, Daisy—yoo-hoo." She knows her name and turns to look at me across the lawn and I wave (feeling ridiculous) and call a few friendly words to her, hoping that it will give her the feeling that she is part of our herd—God knows, it's unstable and haphazard enough for her to feel right at home in.

I had hoped Daisy was about to get a lot of new friends. A week before we left for Malindi she was lying/sitting down in the middle of her launching pad when the warthog family, mother, father, and five youngsters, crossed the lawn in her general direction, pausing from time to time to graze and dig for roots. The weird little band of uglies, walking for the most part on their front knees as is their way when foraging, looked for the moment like a family of amputees on a Sunday outing.

Daisy had her ears pricked up and was watching them intently as they got closer and closer, seemingly oblivious to her presence.

When they were about five paces away she could stand the inexorable advance no longer and scrambled to her feet, an ungainly business even when performed without hurry. The warthogs seemed amazed—could it really be that they had not noticed her? They scuttled off, front limbs miraculously restored, with their tails pointing straight up in the air. Well, I thought, no great friendship there.

A few days later I watched once more as the warthogs advanced, again unknowingly, so it seemed, to where Daisy was chewing her cud quietly under a tree and occasionally nibbling gently at the lower branches. They got closer and closer until they were all under the same tree, Daisy on one side working at the leaves over her head, the warthogs on the other, within a stride of her. Daisy looked down at them once or twice and they up at her, but neither seemed to be paying any real attention to the other. Usually in Africa the nonpredators will mingle with one another, not so much on a friendly basis—I wouldn't put it as high as that—but at least on a mutuality level so long as nobody is disturbing anybody else. And so it seemed now with Daisy and the warthogs. Neither was about to befriend or molest the other, and there was an eight-foot gap separating their areas of primary interest, so she still had no playmates (other than Jock and me). She looked so little and lonely out there all by herself, and she didn't even have a nursery school to be dumped in.

And then I started to worry about how she would know she was a giraffe. She had no mirror—I mean, she may have been starting to think she was a black Labrador. (She may even have been worse off than that dumb albino—he at least knew he was a *giraffe*.) Since there's no giraffe shrink in Nairobi the only way I could think of to solve her identity crisis was—yep, you've guessed it—to get another one.

6

A Star
Is Born

About our fifth evening at Malindi Jock and I were sitting in the living room reading when we heard a plop—a big *plop*. It was a black mamba, the most deadly of snakes and aggressive too, and it had fallen from the *makuti* roof to the floor about a foot from where Shirley Brown was sleeping.

I climbed up on the dining-room table, and fortunately Shirley Brown was more interested in this unusual behavior than in the snake and came over to see where I was going, while Jock and Charo dispatched the mamba. I told Jock that I thought it was an omen—that when black mambas started dropping in it was time to get back to Nairobi. (No, one does *not* see a lot of snakes in Kenya—a lot less than if one were living a rural life in Texas, I'd bet. But at the coast there are a few baddies. Once, when Bobby Kennedy, Jr., was staying in our Malindi house an enormous deadly

125

126

puff adder joined him on the terrace while he was having breakfast. After he killed it, Bobby, who knows about these things, applied skill worthy of a taxidermist and presented us a five-foot skin—huge for a puff adder.)

Anyway, the mamba visit gave us a good excuse to leave earlier than we had planned. We missed Daisy terribly, though we didn't want to admit it to ourselves or each other. Also we were excited about setting up plans to capture a friend for Daisy, since Rutherfurd was due back in civilization the next day from the Northern Province.

Daisy was sooooo happy to see us—she swayed her neck around and did a little skip, then a jump, and ran up to us and kissed and hugged us.

We were secretly delighted to learn that she wouldn't take carrots from our baby-sitter's mouth. The sitter, Marion Gordon (who took many of the photographs in this book and who came to love Daisy in so doing), told us that one evening she was in the stables looking at one of Rick's polo ponies when Tito, who didn't know she was there, came down to the boma to feed Daisy. Then Marion heard this very odd noise. It was Tito imitating me, talking to Daisy in a high-pitched voice, trying to sound like me and saying cutesy things in baby talk—in English yet.

Don't knock it. Listen, at least Daisy will take milk from Tito, who belongs to a tribe for whom milk is not a normal part of the diet, so he doesn't resent her having it and consequently doesn't give off bad vibes, n'est ce pas? By this time we had come to the conclusion that perhaps Daisy's initial rejection of Tito had been because he was frightened of her (though he didn't want to admit as much to us) and his fear made her jumpy.

Anyway, they are now pals and exchanging baby talk, but you'd have to see Tito to appreciate this. He is gargantuan—the ultimate human bulldozer. In a hurry one day I said to him unthinkingly, "Oh, Tito, would you move the car, please?" forgetting he couldn't drive. It didn't faze him at all—he just picked it up by the rear fender and moved it so that another car could get by. Now and again we point him at a valley that needs filling in or a road that has to be cleared through a dense patch of forest, and he tears into the task as if he were made by Caterpillar. When we got back from Malindi Tito said that he was going to quit because Rick had threatened to beat him up.

127

"Why?" I asked.

"Because I was afraid of his horses. He asked me to walk the horses up from the field because the syce was unconscious—"

"Unconscious? Had he fallen from a horse?"

"No, drunk. So I told Rick I was afraid of the horses and that's when he said he was going to beat me up."

"What did you do?"

"I got the horses."

"I thought you were afraid of them."

"I was. But I was more afraid of Rick."

"Of Rick? He's half your size! Are you still afraid of the horses, now that you've handled them and they didn't hurt you?"

"No."

"Then why quit?"

"Oh. All right."

In contrast to his enormous strength and prodigious physical energy, Tito is the most gentle person you could ever hope to meet, as Daisy was finding out.

The syce had evidently been keeping up the image of his profession by drinking himself into a stupor—practically every week Rick fires one and hires another because of it. One syce used to exercise the horses by riding every morning to the Honolulu Bar and then we'd have hysterical calls from neighbors that, on the way back, he had fallen off Quicksilver in the middle of a busy road, once pulling the poor horse down on top of him. When we tried to rescue him and Quicksilver he would fight and end up in jail. His replacement was so drunk a few days later that he mistook a dark bay horse for a car and washed it with foaming detergent. By the time we arrived on this bubble-bath scene he was trying to hose down the endlessly patient horse prior to getting a good shine on it with a chamois leather, but he kept staggering and clutching its tail to steady himself. *His* replacement stole most of our tools and while drunk made the mistake of trying to sell them to the local store which we use. And so it still was going when we returned.

Also, all Langata telephone lines, including ours, had been out of order for two months and we were looking forward to trying the new system which had just been installed while we were away at Malindi. We picked up the telephone to call Rutherfurd to see what he thought about our idea of getting another giraffe, but it was still out of order. Odd for a freshly installed system, we thought. Next day we read in the newspaper that the brand-new copper cables had

128

been stolen by a gang who "took them away to turn into bracelets for tourists or to make fences." (Copper fences?)

Anyway, there was nothing for us to do but drive up to the ranch under Mount Kenya that Rutherfurd was going to run for a few days while the owners were away. After a most elegant candlelit dinner that he prepared for us (he shot the soup himself) we told him of our idea. Sure, he said, great, and once again he set off to walk Douglas and Turbo (Jet) the three days' trip to Lewa Downs, and once again we set about taking the center seat out of the minibus (now known as the Daisybus).

I have a friend who looks like a dandelion—not one of the he-loves-me, he-loves-me-not yellow ones, but a fuzzy one. Her hair sticks out all around her head in a circle of golden see-through pouffs, and she looks as though if you went *pffffff* she'd be left bald on the stem.

My dandelion friend got arrested for measuring. She was on her way out to our house bringing us her Land Rover (named "Twiga," coincidentally), which she had kindly loaned us for the Daisy capture, and she stopped in Nairobi at the Seat-Covers-For-Your-Car shop and double-parked out front. She took out her tape measure and was just scribbling the dimensions on a scrap of paper when a policeman arrived and said, "What are you doing?"

"Measuring," she answered politely, and so next to the offense on the ticket he wrote, "Measuring," and she was fined ten dollars in court when her case came up.

Since she was held up by all this and since our telephone was still out of order and she couldn't reach us, I thought that something had gone wrong with the arrangements and that perhaps she had not understood me clearly when I had telephoned her a few evenings earlier from a friend's apartment. We were not the only ones with telephone problems. Every time Dandelion's telephone rings she has to *run* twenty-five yards outside her house to a tree—where it is situated, for the following reason: When the telephone company came to install her new phone in her house, which was still being built, they made a mistake and put the instrument in a workman's shack in which the builders were storing cement and bricks. When the builders finished they dismantled their shack and took it with them, thus leaving the telephone outside. She had been waiting for two months for the telephone company to come and move it into the house, but they had not yet got around to it, so in the interim she had placed it in a low fork of a nearby tree and hung a piece of canvas over it. When I had called her it was raining heavily, and what with the wind, and the rain, and the flapping canvas, and her puffing after the dash, it wasn't a very clear conversation, so I thought perhaps she had not understood my request to borrow her Land Rover again. I had shouted over the storm something like "We were hoping we could borrow Twiga again," meaning the Land Rover, but maybe she had thought I was talking about getting another *twiga* like Daisy.

Anyway, thinking that there had been a muddle, Jock, Rick, Shirley Brown and I piled into the Daisybus once again and headed for Lewa Downs, hoping that we could do without a four-wheel drive, that the minibus would suffice.

However, on that first evening of cruising around with Rutherfurd, trying to decide which baby to capture and which herd was located on the best terrain for the chase, it became obvious to all of us that we could easily find ourselves in a position the next day, depending on which way the giraffe ran, where the bus would be quite inadequate, and that to be safe we would have to have a four-wheel-drive vehicle as well. Where might we find one?

Rutherfurd knew an Indian, a Sikh mechanic who had a clapped-out Toyota Land Cruiser, and we drove ten miles into Eldoret to find him. In his back yard were half a dozen broken-down trucks and rusty-looking vehicles and, in one corner, what looked like a professional hunter's wagon all fitted up with gunracks and roof hatches. Most hunters have two or three of these to take their clients into the bush, and they are usually painted a drab green and have semi-open sides and backs so that you can get in and out in a hurry, and there are often canvas curtains which are kept rolled up except when it rains. David Craig owns one on his other ranch and calls it his Hemingway vehicle because male tourists, particularly, undergo some weird metamorphosis when they first sit in such hunt-ing cars, and before they have gone a mile they have given up shaving and are looking around for a bottle from which to swig raw liquor. These vehicles do have a certain *class*, but the one we be-held, while conforming to the pattern, had the whole effect spoiled by having "Jungle Fever" in bright yellow letters painted on the back. (You are meant to feel the jungle fever without having to be *told* you are feeling it.)

The Sikh's son was working on a truck and said that we would have to talk to his father about renting Jungle Fever. We knocked on the door and a pretty daughter in a sari answered and said that she would call her father. We waited and waited until a cheerful, portly Sikh with a salt-and-pepper beard and fuchsia turban stepped out, and then we haggled for thirty minutes about the rate. Usually cars are hired on a mileage formula, but since we would be doing such a relatively low mileage on a nearby ranch, he wished instead to put the deal on a massive daily-rate basis. Americans are inclined to find this kind of bargaining very tedious, and I also hate it be-cause I am terrible at it. Not only does it seem to me to be a waste of time, but I always figure the guy in rags with open sores selling me the carved elephant needs the one shilling more than I do.

But Indians and many people who have lived in Kenya for a long time, like Jock and Rutherfurd, simply accept that this kind of bar-gaining is a game, a minor art form, where everybody gives ground from his initial position to arrive at the final formula. There is seldom animosity and the whole thing is a sort of structured social exchange. The Sikh was better at the game than either Jock or Rutherfurd. We drove off in the expensive thing hoping that none of our friends would see us riding around in Jungle Fever.

The cottage which the Craigs loaned us at Soy was simple but charming. It sat in a tree-filled hollow near a dam and looked like a Hansel and Gretel house. The kitchen was a separate little building and just beyond that were the servants' quarters, where their cook, Jonathan, lived with his pretty young wife and three small children.

At night we had a choice of starting a little portable motor out back which ran a generator of just sufficient power to operate a light bulb in each room or, if we didn't feel like fighting the engine, of using candles and one or two bright gas lamps which we had brought with us.

The water ran from the taps all right, but it looked like minestrone, having been pumped directly from the dam. It was heated in typical Kenya fashion in a forty-gallon oil drum under which Jonathan kept a huge wood fire roaring from about six o'clock every evening.

Since the Craigs no longer used the cottage and were winding down the ranch in preparation for the takeover by the new settlers, they had just moved out all the furniture, so this time we had brought basic necessities with us: mattresses which we placed on the floor in the bedrooms, six campstools, and a large upturned cardboard box which became our dining table. That was it.

Jonathan was very concerned at what he took to be the depths of discomfort in which we had to live, though we didn't mind at all, and it was certainly a lot easier than camping. He bustled about doing his best to see that our needs were taken care of.

After making one more check in Jungle Fever on the giraffe herd we had selected, we drove back to the cottage. Rutherfurd came in and took some yellow embroidery thread out of his pocket.

"Going to work on your needlepoint?" I asked him.

He didn't answer, of course, but started assembling three or four lengths of rope which, assuming we were successful, would be needed the following day to tie up the baby's feet. He also devised two sliding nooses to go around the neck, each with a large knot to prevent the noose from tightening beyond a certain point and throttling the poor thing. He used his pretty thread to lash the catching rope onto a stick.

"Someone must have been hunting them," Rutherfurd said. "They're very nervous and skittish."

We speculated that perhaps the incoming farmers were getting really impatient and were stepping up their efforts to rid the land of the game. We knew, though none of us said it out loud, that the Rothschild would be much more alert than when we had caught Daisy—much harder to get close to—and that therefore it would entail a faster and even more dangerous gallop than ever to get in among them.

Rutherfurd doesn't know, and won't ever know perhaps unless he reads this book, that Jock took out an insurance policy on him in case he ended up badly injured in a hospital or even crippled. Lloyds of London were the only people who would cover it—$100 for a fifteen-minute chase. (He'll be as mad as hell. "Bloody waste of money!" he'll say.)

I was upset and uneasy about all the risks involved, now that I understood them better after the Daisy capture, and hardly slept at all that night.

It started off as the same old movie—starring Rutherfurd and Douglas and Kiborr and Turbo (Jet) in *Mission Impossible*.

They set out as if they were going for a nice little horseback ride in the park on a Sunday morning. We followed in Jungle Fever, and this time we had two cameramen and the Gordons along to film the chase and the capture. As Rutherfurd trotted off with the loop of rope dangling from his stick, his friend Ken McBride, who had the job of winding down Lewa Downs, laughed and called out so that Rutherfurd could hear, "He looks as if he's going off to hang himself." I feared that the outcome might amount to the same thing.

Just as in the first capture, we rendezvoused at a prearranged spot while Rutherfurd selected his target. About a hundred yards to the left of the herd stood a mother and baby by themselves, both eating from thorn bushes. "That's the one," he said, and off he and Kiborr went at full tilt. Evidently he figured that the giraffe were nervous anyway and that there was nothing to be gained from the gentle approach he had used first time around. As we watched we could see he had something else in mind, too: to cut out the mother and baby right away before they could seek the security of the herd. The ploy worked beautifully and the chase speeded up with Kiborr and

133

Rutherfurd already closing on the baby without having had to fight their way through the herd.

But even though they had saved themselves one hair-raising step the little thing had plenty of energy and in a minute the galloping giraffes, mother and baby, with the horses fifty yards to the rear, had disappeared from sight, lost behind thick bush. It was like having the same recurring nightmare, a kind of ominous *déjà vu*, as we tagged along as best we could, trying to catch up. After what seemed like an interminable time of bouncing and banging in the rattling safari car over terrain boobytrapped by ant bears, Rutherfurd came into view ahead of us, looking exhausted, on a sweat-soaked Douglas. But this time he said, "It's a boy."

Rutherfurd retraced his steps and we followed as well as we could. Then suddenly we came round a clump of bush and there it was. A tiny baby. He still had his umbilical cord and was therefore only about three weeks old, and he looked a little like Bambi or some other Walt Disney adorable. We could see right away how different he was from Daisy. Not only was he smaller, but he was a much lighter color and had a very different face. As Rick pointed out, he

134

136

looked sort of Chinese: his eyes seemed far apart and had a slight slant to them. I guess I had expected all giraffe to look alike, and certainly to be alike, but everything about him, including his personality, we were to learn, was entirely different.

Rutherfurd said that before he started the chase he had thought the baby was older, because he was definitely eating leaves—we had all seen that—and they don't usually start browsing until they are about six weeks old. Right there we should have been tipped off that he would be precocious, but for now we were entranced with his being so little and babylike. I went up to him and touched him; he felt like a pussy willow. Then I gave him a big kiss and sweet words and fell in love all over again.

Suddenly, a motion in the bushes behind us caused us all to look round, and there, very close, stood his mother peering down at her son. She looked bewildered and helpless and just stood there watch-

ing and wondering what was happening to him, what could she do and how would she ever get her baby back.

It was just too sad for me to endure, and but for the arrival of the Daisybus at that moment I would have said to let him go. "This is his only chance of survival, " Jock tried to comfort me.

Instead of the terrible kicking and roping and throwing and fighting we had been through with Daisy, four people simply picked this baby up as if he were a Great Dane and put him in the bus, where Kiborr held his head up as we drove gently back to the stables. Getting him into the stall was a bit of a fighting hassle, but once inside he just stood there, as Daisy had, with the difference that he didn't seem to be panicking, but plotting. (See plotting expression in photo at beginning of chapter.) He stood sideways in the stable staring straight at the blank wall and refused to look at us. When I stopped telling him how beautiful he was and looked away from him for a minute he'd sneak a glance at me out of the corner of his eye, but the second I'd turn back he would look away quickly, pretending he hadn't peeped at all. How I dreaded the next four days of won-

dering if he would be alive each morning, holding the pan of milk and not having him drink.

Once again Rutherfurd said that the best thing was to leave him alone and suggested a beer—to which nobody objected.

The cameramen had got the chase on film, but not the capture. Not only were they disturbed by the fact that they had missed the crucial part, but they had not realized that it would be so hair-raising and were somewhat shattered, as were we, by the strain of the whole adventure. We all headed for the Soy Club.

On the way Rutherfurd said to me, "I'll get another one this afternoon and let it go. Perhaps they can get the capture footage then."

"You really *are* crazy, aren't you? Your chances of killing yourself are—"

"Look, I'm only doing it for you and Jock."

"Do you think that makes me feel any *better*? No, I don't want you to."

When we arrived at the Club, Ken was waiting there and greeted Rutherfurd with a surprised smile. "You still alive?"

Rutherfurd took a swig of nice warm beer and said to the cameramen, "At four this afternoon we do it again."

The happiest one about the repeat performance was Douglas. Rutherfurd had said that unless Douglas was capturing giraffe he was bored, and that afternoon, more than delighted by the surprise of doing it twice in one day, he was prancing around quite over-come by himself and looking more like a circus horse than ever. Turbo (Jet) was almost drooling as he admired Douglas' every move.

Again the same nightmare—like Cecil B. De Mille shooting the same cavalry charge over and over, but this was for real. Rutherfurd and Kiborr drowned in a herd of running, kicking giraffe, separated a baby, chased it, and were just on the point of closing in to wrestle it to the ground when Jungle Fever went into an ant-bear hole and the cameramen simply couldn't get there in time. Rutherfurd let the little thing run back to its mother, then trotted up on Douglas to where Jungle Fever was stuck.

"I'll catch another one tomorrow—you'll get it on film then," he said.

"Why don't you just get a gun and shoot yourself?" I shouted at him, and I went back to the stable and sulked with the baby giraffe for the rest of the evening.

As I closed the top half of the stable door before returning to the cottage for another sleepless night, I begged him, "You're such a sweet baby, please don't die."

At dawn Jock did the inspection and came running back, calling happily to Rick and me that the giraffe was fine but wait till we saw what he had done to his bedroom. We made our way to the stable and you should have seen the shambles. We had left a pan of water there, and he had kicked it from one end of the stable to the other and then flattened it. The bales of hay which we had stacked five high around the walls for padding had been ripped down and were broken apart, and the mass of loose straw was piled all over the floors so that it was like a water bed when he walked on it—all resilient in the wrong places and uneven, and it made him stagger comically. He stood there, perky and alert and proud of his demolition work, but he still wouldn't look at us and continued to stare at the wall, just every now and then sneaking that occasional glance out of the corner of his eye. In what I assumed would be a useless effort I held the milk pan for him right under his nose, and he put his head in it to see what it was. He got one gulp, I think, but most of it went up his nose, over his face, in his eyelashes, some even on his horns, and he stood there letting the rest drip all over me. But he still wouldn't look at me.

I held it out again and he put his head in again, and he managed to suck some up this time, but only after making another terrible mess all over both of us. Then he stared at the wall. No saying thank you, no kisses. But curiosity was his weakness, and finally after two hours he turned and looked at me. He had such a cute face and such an odd expression that I laughed, and I still laugh with delight twenty-five times every day when I see him.

We were so happy with him and with the fact that he had drunk on the morning of the second day instead of keeping us in a state of nervous tension for three days as Daisy had done.

From time to time he would stand on his rear legs, with his front feet on a broken bale of straw, looking like a gerunuk (a type of long-necked antelope) but acting like Houdini—a sneaky Houdini, at that: he would regard us with a slight frown and, pretending to like us, would come over to where we were standing by the stable door as if to let us touch him, but instead he would lunge at the open top half of the door, heading out. We'd grab him by his neck and head and shove him back and he'd then eye us cunningly for a while before starting the whole escape procedure again.

As the day wore on he couldn't resist looking at us more often,

141

and soon he came up and gently put his face next to mine and let me touch him for the first time. Just when he saw how I melted and how much I was enjoying caressing his soft downy nose, he lunged again at the opening, almost knocking me down in his effort to get out. He kept repeating the same procedure, getting us to lower our guard by being sweet and then making another attempt at jailbreaking.

What an actor! And so beautiful! We named him Marlon. As in Brando.

Rutherfurd arrived right before the time set for the third capture, and, seeing that Marlon was in fine shape, he said, "You know Suzannah—my giraffe—whom I haven't seen for three years since I left here?"

"The one who ate your soap out of your bathroom window?" Rick asked.

"That's right."

"Well, Suzannah is this twiga's mother."

"What are you talking about?" we asked.

"Well, yesterday, during the chase I thought it was odd that the mother didn't start to run when she saw me approaching. She let me and Douglas get unusually close. Then, I've never seen one stay around during the capture and for all that time afterwards. You remember how with Daisy there wasn't another giraffe in sight? They always take off. Yet you saw how this one's mother was there for what—half an hour yesterday? I was beginning to think something was peculiar, and then this morning the night herdsman said that Suzannah came *here* to the stables last night. He knows her because of a mark on her ear."

"Why didn't you tell us what you suspected yesterday?" I asked.

"Because I thought if—what's his name, Marlon?—if Marlon died, and the odds were quite heavy that he might, you'd really be upset, taking Suzannah's baby away from her and all that."

I was distraught.

"Look," he said, "he'd be dead in two months if we didn't have him now, just don't forget that. Think of it as our having *saved* Suzannah's baby."

Then we learned something that we were to reflect upon often in the months that followed. There are scientists who believe that giraffe may be able to communicate by means of ultrasonics in the way that bats do, by emitting some high-pitched signal beyond the range of the human ear. It just so happens that we picked up a piece of admittedly slim evidence to corroborate the theory, and we got it

142

from the night herdsman who had been looking after a herd of steers which had been brought into the corral the evening before. We had asked him to check on Marlon during the night, just to make sure he was O.K.

Marlon had been relatively calm when we left him at 9 P.M., but the herdsman told us that around midnight he had heard him trying to get out. Upon checking, he found that Marlon was making his escape bid up against the solid brick wall at the rear, not through the door at the front of the stable, which was made of rough boards and had large chinks that he could see through, and which would have been the logical route to try for an exit. The herdsman then continued his patrol a hundred yards or more away from the stables and in the moonlight spotted a lone giraffe, which stayed approximately in the same place until dawn, when he recognized her as Suzannah.

The interesting thing about this is that the place where Suzannah had been standing was directly behind the rear brick wall of the stables, though some distance away. There is nothing odd about her tracking down her child by scent, and indeed the steady wind that night would have carried his scent to the point where she was standing. But if that was the case, the wind could not have carried her scent in the opposite direction to Marlon, yet it was obvious to the herdsman that Marlon knew she was there—though not a sound was uttered. Those who have spent a lot of time watching giraffe herds in the wild believe that they have a rudimentary form of semaphore going, and that they can give signals to one another over great distances. Obvious signals would be neck movements, or holding the neck in a particular position, and tail switching, but Marlon was indoors and he and his mother could definitely not see each other. If the ultrasonics theory has any validity, then there would seem to be no need for physical signals. However it is done, giraffe buffs are in agreement that giraffe are able to communicate.

"It really is an incredible coincidence that I happened to single out Suzannah's baby," said Rutherfurd, "but you should be glad about it. For a start, she had a super personality, so Marlon probably will have one, too, and secondly, since only about thirty out of one hundred and eighty will be rescued, the odds were against either of them being alive for long." Then he glanced at his watch. "Let's go."

This time the herd was in a shallow valley and the plan was that the horsemen would approach from the opposite edge and go down into the valley so that the cameramen could get the action coming towards them. Cameras were poised and ready for the third capture.

I refused to stay. Let the consenting idiots kill themselves; I didn't have to watch again. As I was driving away from the scene where the crime was likely to take place, winding around on a dirt track, trying to find my way back to the stable, whom did I unwittingly bump into but Rutherfurd and Kiborr on their horses, waiting for Jock to give the signal from a mile away that the cameramen were ready and in place.

"We don't *have* to have the capture on film, you know. If it's a rough and cruel-looking business it might not be suitable for audiences anyway," I lied to Rutherfurd in a last attempt to dissuade him. "Won't you change your mind?"

Just then, on the far side, Jock signaled.

"No," Rutherfurd called, clutching his stick as he galloped down the slope towards the giraffe. And Kiborr came tumbling after. As they both reached full speed going downhill into the herd, and as the giraffe were starting to move in their enormous galloping stride towards the hidden cameramen, Turbo (Jet) went into an ant-bear hole, taking a tremendous spill of the kind I had been dreading all along. Kiborr flew off over his head landing on the ground yards from his horse. Miraculously, though, within a few seconds both rider and horse were up, and neither appeared to be hurt. But Turbo (Jet) had had enough and refused to be caught, taking off in the opposite direction, not to be seen again that day. Without Kiborr to keep the giraffe in line and herded back towards Rutherfurd they started to mill and wheel all over the place, so the attempt had to be abandoned.

I was delighted. Even the cameramen, although disappointed not to have filmed an actual capture, seemed relieved that the risky undertakings had ended. With hopes that they had much exciting footage anyway, they left for Nairobi, but Marion and Don Gordon who were taking stills and sharing the cottage with us stayed on, and we had two lazy days of walking up and down to the stables looking at Marlon, our Chinese giraffe (could it be that a *tsu-la* forebear of his had somehow made his way *back* from China?), and waiting for him to gain strength enough for his trip to Nairobi. Although he spent every minute running around trying to escape and kicked out two entire boards from one side of his stall, he didn't seem nearly as traumatized by his capture as Daisy had been. He was just determined to get the hell out of there. One time when I went to see him he was standing up on his rear legs again, peering over into the next stall, looking for a way out that way, and I was afraid he would hurt his legs or get them caught in the broken wooden boards. But since we couldn't go in with him there was no way we could physically stop him from breaking the place apart, so I decided to frame him with a little distracting device. I cut an end off a thorn-tree branch, stuck sliced carrots on each thorn, and held out the branch so that he could see it. For about five minutes he stared at it in wonder. He recognized the thorn-tree branch immediately, but he had never seen those round orange things growing on one before. Of course he simply could not resist having a closer look and then trying it. Since he had never eaten anything like that, he didn't know what to do with a carrot slice once he had it in his mouth, and he reminded me of Daisy, jiggling his head up and down as he tried to chew, throwing bits of carrot flying over his head or onto the ground in front of him.

He was just too young to handle carrots yet, but he was intrigued with the goings-on. I then held some pieces out to him, but of course he didn't know how to take them from my hand, and he didn't really want to eat them anyway, but all day he pretended to be interested in order to get closer to me. He investigated my fingers, my hands, and then he'd take a carrot slice off a thorn and play with it, pretending to eat it, but actually he'd spit it out. I would hold the carrots on a stick closer to my face, and he'd peek through the twigs, and our noses would touch and then I'd sneak a kiss. He liked it. More and more he wanted me to touch him, and two days later he was kissing me back. He also learned to drink properly and was becoming hooked on carrots—or the carrot game, rather, because he still couldn't cope with them. And since I was becoming his milk and carrot pusher, I was gaining power over him. God bless carrots—we couldn't make our giraffe do *anything* if it weren't for carrots.

Possibly because we had captured him when he was so young, Marlon adapted much more quickly than Daisy and had lost his fear of us within forty-eight hours. The whole transition from wild baby giraffe to well-adjusted captive had been infinitely easier than with Daisy, and Marlon seemed determined to enjoy himself whatever came along.

Each morning Jock and Don Gordon drove together to Eldoret to get milk for Marlon. (We were not giving him the farm milk but buying pasteurized milk from town in order to prevent him from getting sick like Daisy.) One afternoon we all drove to town. As we crossed the railroad track Don Gordon said, "We had to stop and wait for the train here yesterday."

"You had a *big day!*" exclaimed Marion.

The Gordons left that evening to return to Nairobi, but they should have hung around for one more day, because that's when things *really* began to happen.

On the evening of their departure a very polite and pleasant Game Scout appeared at Marlon's stall and wanted to know what we were doing. Jock said that he was surprised to see a representative of the Game Department on private land, but it turned out that he had been posted there specially to try to keep the poaching in check as the settlers readied themselves and moved onto the land. The fact that he turned up so promptly seemed to indicate that he was trying to do a good job of protecting the giraffe which had been given into his charge.

Luckily Jock had brought with him the letter from the Chief Game Warden's office in Nairobi giving us permission to capture both Daisy and Marlon, but the Scout was insistent that Jock should write a note to the Divisional Game Warden in Kapenguria saying that we had accomplished what we had come to do, and giving all the appropriate references from our letter of permission so that things could be verified. It was quite an impressive show of efficiency. Having no paper "to hand," as Jock says (he often talks like Hamlet), he asked the Scout to come down to the cottage in an hour or so, after we had fed Marlon.

When Jock had the note ready he took it out to the Game Scout who was chatting with Jonathan and his wife by the kitchen. The Scout saluted very smartly, folded the envelope neatly into an official-looking book which he was carrying, and departed.

The following morning Jock got up early, as he usually does, and walked the mile to the stables to see how Marlon was. Rick and I remained asleep, but in half an hour or so we were up, too, having breakfast. The cottage was isolated and so I was surprised to hear a terrific commotion outside, with raised voices and running. Within a second Jonathan burst in and beckoned urgently for us to come. Out by the kitchen two men were holding his wife, who was clutching one terrified baby, while two younger children huddled under a tree nearby, screaming. As we watched, Jonathan rushed towards his wife, pulled her away from the men and shoved her roughly into

146

his house, slamming the door behind her and locking it. The two men started after him and while one of them held him the other wrenched open the door and dragged the girl out again. Rick and I shouted for them to stop, and amazingly enough they did. The children continued to scream and the woman went back into the house, while Jonathan and the two men came up to where Rick and I were standing and all started to talk at once, very loudly.

When I first moved to live in Kenya I went to a language school run by missionaries and learned Swahili. I completed the three-month course satisfactorily and have been able to get along ever since with everyday Swahili, but I am by no means an expert in the language and have a hard time understanding when it is spoken at 100 r.p.m. with the volume turned right up. Also the missionaries never taught me the word for "adultery," which turned out to be the key to this conversation. Rick was not much help, because it is only latterly that he has moved to Kenya permanently and his Swahili isn't even as good as mine. As far as we could gather the two men were trying to tell us that Jonathan's wife was their sister, that they had come to take her away, and would we call the police. Tempers were getting out of hand again and Jonathan and the men started threatening each other, so Rick quietly armed himself with a *panga* (machete) while I went to the stables to get Jock, who has had a lifetime of experience in coping with *shauris* (rows) of this kind, which are very commonplace in Africa. Woman's lib isn't exactly big in rural Kenya, and as a woman I lacked any authority in their eyes. As for Rick, in addition to his Swahili not being up to it he was a bit young. The older a man is, the more he is listened to and respected.

I explained to Jock what had been happening with Jonathan, and when Jock stepped out of the car, wearing his "elder" face, he told them he wasn't interested in hearing about it until he had had a cup of coffee, which he asked Jonathan to bring. He told the other two to sit by the tree and the woman to stop her children from crying.

Jock spoke Swahili before English and is as fluent as if he were an African, and that too carries much weight, for they reason that if you know so much about the language it is likely that you are conversant with other matters of local interest, including the resolution of shauris at cook and gardener level—and they reason right. Jock never raised his voice but simply stated what was going to happen, and everyone fell into line. After his coffee he went out and quietly heard each person's story in turn. Looking through the window

147

from time to time, I could see that he appeared to be very earnest, but when he caught my eye it was obvious that he found the shauri of the amusing rather than the serious variety.

What had happened was this: The efficient Game Scout of the day before had spied Jonathan's pretty wife and had taken a fancy to her—as she had to him, evidently. The evening before, they had somehow arranged a little assignation and she had scurried up to his house and had been surprised *in flagrante* by Jonathan, who must have been suspicious. Instead of beating up the Game Scout, he knocked his wife about and she ran off to tell her brothers that she was married to a wicked wife-beating husband. They then turned up at the cottage to take her home to Mother, but Jonathan had no intention of losing her, so it seemed. She too had second thoughts about leaving (it might have crossed her mind that if she went home to Mother she would not be able to see the Game Scout again).

The brothers were insisting that the police be called to resolve all this, but Jock explained that adultery was not actually a criminal offense, and that unless she wished to bring charges against Jonathan for beating her up there was no part for the police to play. The whole thing started to get very confused as the various antagonists shifted their ground after having heard what each of the others had to say, and Jonathan, who had started off by wanting to keep his wife, now wanted instead to hand her over to the police for being an adultress. One of the brothers resolved to charge Jonathan with assault for beating up his sister, but the other brother thought that they should stick to Plan No. 1., which was taking the sister home, but that in addition the Game Scout should be charged for stealing her away from Jonathan. Having said this, he realized it looked as though he were siding with Jonathan, so he wound up his argument with a confused statement about Jonathan's unsuitability as a husband, otherwise why would his wife be running around with Game Scouts?

Nobody asked or even considered what the girl thought about it all.

Jock knew that the whole day, and probably the next day as well, could be given over to this momentous problem, so he decided to end the matter. The wife, he said, would stay with Jonathan. The brothers would go home or back to their jobs, and Jonathan would devote his energies to planning what we were going to have for lunch.

It has never ceased to amaze me how Jock, and others who have been in Kenya a long time, can get away with this. Probably it is because they don't go around interfering in people's lives, but rather they are simply there, and arguing parties actually come to them seeking arbitration, wanting a decision from a neutral. The two brothers stood up and smiled as if they had won their point and seemed relieved that it was all over. Jonathan smiled also and seemed very satisfied, and his wife wandered off aimlessly with the children as if none of the last twenty-four hours had happened. (Or maybe she was weaving her way back to the Game Scout's pad.)

The next day, though, when we arrived back at the cottage, we saw that one of the brothers was waiting for us.

Okay, said Jock, what's the matter, why aren't you happy to leave things as they are?

Oh no, he explained, it was nothing to do with all that sister foolishness, nothing at all. But the thought had occurred to him that if we were interested in giraffe we would probably be interested also in buying an elephant tusk at a very reasonable price.

Knowing that the tusk must have come from a poached elephant, since Government is the only body allowed to handle ivory legally, we said, cannily, that although we ourselves were not interested in ivory transactions we knew certain people who were and would make inquiries. We refrained from telling him that our friends were in the antipoaching unit of the Game Department.

The next day he was back again, this time with an extremely smart-looking gentleman in an impeccably pressed and laundered official uniform of the Railways, with a highly polished brass insignia reading "Station Master." After the usual courtesies had been exchanged the stationmaster told us that since his friend had revealed as how we might be interested in ivory, he knew where we could obtain some gold at a very reasonable rate, and diamonds also, though not being a specialist he could not be sure what the particular stones were. The Mines and Geological Department maintain a very tight hold, through a series of concessions grated to licensed prospectors, and it was so patently obvious to all of us, even the stationmaster, that he was not such a person that we tacitly skated around the question of legality. Here we were, 225 miles into the bush for the purpose of acquiring one legal giraffe, and within forty-eight hours the locals were trying to offload onto us poached ivory, illicit gold, and hot gemstones.

We toyed with the idea of getting in touch with the police in order to lure the brother with his tusk and the happy stationmaster with his gold and diamonds into a trap, but we didn't. Knowing the distribution of elephant in the area, we figured that the most likely place where the tusk had come from was on the Uganda side of Mount Elgon and it was hardly probable that one would get much satisfaction by complaining to Big Daddy Amin about that. The dealing in gold and diamonds at stationmaster level is usually so petty, and the amounts so small, that it is barely worth the fuss of a court case. The Criminal Investigation Department is better utilized in checking up on biggies in Nairobi and, indeed, in examining the very system which grants licenses that "legalize" monumental ripoffs. At the level of a stationmaster or a cook's brother-in-law one can be reasonably certain that Rockefeller-sized fortunes are not changing hands.

On the morning of departure I got to the stable to see Marlon before anyone else and there stood an African with a great big shotgun, and he was not wearing either a police or an army uniform. Guns are very strictly licensed in Kenya, so this was a rare and spooky sight.

"What are you going to do with that?" I asked.

"Shoot it."

"Shoot what?"

"People," he answered.

"What people?"

"Nandi."

"Oh," I said.

He was a Meru by tribe and didn't like the Nandi much, and he relished shooting them, so he'll probably get quite a few, since Soy is right on the edge of Nandi territory. Cattle thieves—that's what it's all about. The Government allows stock farmers to arm their herdsmen, because rustling is such a major problem that at times it threatens a national industry. Some of the tribes like the Maasai and the Samburu look on rustling more as a sport than as anything else, and the fact that it's not allowed and that you can be killed if you are caught in the act only makes it more fun for young warriors who are dying (no pun) to flex themselves. So long as a herdsman can show that the rustler he shot was armed and driving cattle away, that's usually the end of the matter.

When I got back to the cottage Jonathan approached me to ask a favor. Would we please give him two hundred shillings to get his wife out of jail? Jail? Yes, jail, he answered, chagrined. Since we

150

were just leaving to take Marlon to Nairobi we hadn't time to talk about it, and anyhow we decided we would rather not know why she was in jail, so we coughed up the two hundred shillings. Back in Nairobi, we considered the possibility that the whole thing had been a setup—that perhaps the wife, the brothers, and Jonathan enact this little soap opera for everyone who stays in the Hansel and Gretel cottage. It's a good way for them to earn twenty-five dollars.

What a crazy spot—like an open-air mental hospital, or an African *Peyton Place:* "And so, ladies and gentlemen, tune in this time next week, 1230 on your radio dial, to see if Marlon is still alive, if the cook's wife is out of jail or back in bed with the Game Scout. Will the brothers save her again? What if the Game Scout discovers they are selling ivory? skins? diamonds? How many Nandi has the Meru shot? Yes, folks, don't forget to tune in for the next exciting episode in . . . (drums in background) *Jungle Fever!*"

The plan for Marlon's trip back to Nairobi was a replica of the one for Daisy's trip: Rick and Jock and Kiborr and Marlon would ride in the Daisybus, and Rutherfurd and I would follow in his car.

This is where we can blow the myth that giraffe can't make any noise. When Rutherfurd and his team went into the stall to rope him, Marlon let out a sound that was a cross between the moo of a cow and a fierce roar, and about as loud. It startled everyone and nearly scared me to death. It was the only time any of us had ever heard that noise. However, he made mooing grunts frequently after that.

Looking forward to having fun surprising the gas station attendants again, Jock drove in to fill up, but before they could even get close enough to see Marlon they called to Jock, "Ah, Jambo Bwana, got another giraffe?" We shouldn't have been surprised; Africans remember everything, and it was only four months since we had come by with Daisy. That was Thanksgiving and now it was April— which makes Daisy a Virgo and Marlon an Aries. Anxious to see how they would get along, I looked up what an astrologer thought about the combination of Virgo and Aries. "This match with your opposite sign can work out well, provided Virgo remembers Aries need tenderness and an open avowal of love."

Hoping Daisy had read this, too, we drove into our driveway tense with anticipation about their encounter. Stiff from his ride, Marlon wobbled into the boma like a drunk when we unloaded him, and seemed really pleased to see Daisy. And poor little lonely Daisy, for

151

whom we had gone to all this trouble just so that she could have a friend to make her happy, walked up to him and kicked him. Hard.

7

May I Have
Your Autogiraffe?

We had had to build a new house for the new baby and had decided that the best thing would be to put up another little slatted house within the boma close to Daisy's bedroom, so that they could be near and could touch each other through the bars if they wanted, yet have privacy.

What better person to undertake this than our crooked friend Kiarie, who had built Daisy's Place? Nearly ten years earlier Kiarie had first showed up on our doorstep, as is the way in Africa, a tall ragged figure with a winning smile and all the airs of a con artist. He wanted a job, he said, and would do anything. How about cutting the branch off that tall tree? he suggested, adding cryptically that it looked as if with the next rainstorm it might fall and damage that end of the house.

We told him we would risk it. What about putting tarmac on the

driveway, then? No, we told him, the driveway was fine as it was, and really we had no job for him.

Anybody with a property in Nairobi is faced with this situation at least twice a week, because unemployment is high and many jobless Africans suffer terribly. "High" means over ninety percent, but in Africa that is not comparable to a Western country. While only ten percent of our population here may be relying for survival on wages or salaries, the balance live a life of peasant agriculture, growing what they need for themselves and their families on five- to ten-acre plots, building their houses out of sticks and mud and thatch, and drawing their water from a river or a lake. Some do quite well this way and have surplus cash crops to sell, but as Kenya's population expands there is less and less arable land available, and more young people flock to the cities in search of jobs. But the cities are not sufficiently industrialized, and hundreds of thousands of Africans wait helplessly with no shamba (farm) in their home areas and no job in the towns. It is amazing that more do not turn to crime, because their needs are so desperate. Knowing this, one tries to be as gentle and sympathetic as possible when telling somebody that one has no job for him.

Kiarie was not in the least deterred when we told him that there was nothing we could give him to do. He arrived merrily at our house almost every morning anyway and stayed all day long, just watching other people work—in the garden, in the house—and giving much friendly and unsolicited advice.

He had an unusually direct manner. If we were having a conversation with a contractor, say, he would join the group and listen with great interest, and later he would ask us how much we were being charged and tell us that it was too high and that he knew someone better who would do it at a cheaper rate. Years later when we sold that house he wanted to know how much we had asked for it, how much we got, how much we paid for our new house, and asked many other astonishing questions that our friends would not have had the gall to ask. I was equally astonished to find that I was not in the least offended and gave answers easily, simply because Kiarie's was not a gossipy curiosity, but merely his way of learning what the *wazungu*'s world was all about. He could neither read nor write, but he had a great natural intelligence and a tremendous desire to learn. If anyone should have been educated it was Kiarie; he might have been head of the Police Force by now, or certainly someone really exciting like Al Capone.

One day he cast a professional eye over our lawn, where he spotted some fresh molehills. "Why do you allow the moles to ruin the otherwise beautiful lawn?" he asked.

"Our own gardener can trap them perfectly well with a bent stick, a piece of string, and a tin can," we told him. If that was the case, why hadn't the gardener rid us of the unsightly moles? asked Kiarie, pointing out three fresh mounds that we hadn't noticed until then.

In the face of such salesmanship we weaken easily. We told him that he could have a go at the moles and that he would find the string in the toolshed. Kiarie laughed and shook his head. He wasn't one to catch moles by such pathetically unreliable methods, he explained; he would be back the next day with a special poisonous plant which he would bury in their burrows, and that would be the last we would see of the moles. Jock says moles are a part of life and lawns, but they were new to me—there aren't many in Baltimore. Sure enough, next day Kiarie was back with some innocent-looking green stalks which he proceeded to insert carefully into the tunnels between various molehills, and he said that would be twenty shillings please.

Jock asked what kind of fool he took him for and told him that he wanted evidence, or rather lack of evidence, in the shape of no further molehills. That was fine by Kiarie, who said that he would certainly accept deferred payment. Three days later when Jock returned from the office Kiarie insisted he take an evening walk around the lawn with him. Where were the fresh molehills? he asked. Jock poked around for a bit and had to confess that there were none.

The next time he popped up we talked in the driveway, and just as Jock was telling him that this time there was *really* nothing for him to do we found ourselves standing among a mass of safari ants which climbed up our legs and bit us with the sharp pincers on their heads. It is very funny to watch someone else being attacked, and by exactly inverse ratio unfunny when attacked oneself. We often have groups of tourists out to our house for coffee and a talk, and more than once, as they admired Kilimanjaro from our lawn, a dozen staid people from Iowa and retired Florida couples have been galvanized into the most amazing contortions. Rigid bankers have been known to whip their pants off in public, and lady librarians to do revealing things, as they scrabble to pick off the ants. When Kiarie and we had divested ourselves of the ants and recovered our composure, I saw him smile and sensed what was coming. Had he seen the ants as he arrived on our property and deliberately engaged us in conversation in the very spot where we would be attacked?

Why didn't we allow him to get rid of them? he now suggested. All that he would have to do would be to trace the column back to the main nest, which must be somewhere on our property, and he would dig them out, removing the queen ants whose presence are the reason for the existence of the colony. Without them, he assured us, the other ants would disperse and would set up a new colony somewhere else, probably on our neighbor's property. He laughed and I could see the way his mind worked, chasing ant colonies back and forth among the neighbors over the years and assuring himself a steady run of work in the queen-ant business. We certainly didn't know how to get rid of the ants, and our gardener said that he had no intention of finding out, so early next morning Kiarie started on the nest, which he had tracked down with uncanny skill, and I must say we genuflected to him. The pit he dug was three feet deep by six feet wide, and inside it was a seething mass of angry black ants. Standing ankle deep in them, he confessed that they were biting him, but he persisted anyway and removed nine queens which looked like revolting white slugs. The whole procedure was so fascinating that we filmed it.

The safari ants, or *siafu*, will attack living creatures of any size when they are in the mood. For most animals, including man, they are simply a painful nuisance rather than a threat, because all you have to do is move away a few paces and pick or brush them off, and the bite is not toxic—it is simply a piercing nip. However, a tiny baby or a dog on a chain could be devoured by the ants. For a giraffe or a horse the ants *per se* are not a danger, but the discomfort they inflict could cause panic if the animal felt trapped in the stable, and it could hurt itself trying to escape. Some of the more primitive Africans living in remote areas make use of the large warrior ants in a very clever way. If a man cuts himself he will squeeze the two edges of the cut together and will capture a large ant, which he then holds in position so that the pincers bite astride the wound. Then he will tweak off the body, leaving the head and the pincers as a perfect suture. I'm told that they also exude formic acid, which has healing properties.

Kiarie, a great backwoodsman, knew all of this and much more about the ants. At the end of the day as he was returning the shovel and the pickax to the toolshed, he scratched his head wearily and told us something which we already knew: the toolshed was too

157

small for our accumulation of mowers, sacks of cement, ladders, tires, half-full and empty tins of paint, and all the useless things one keeps in such a place. . . .

The new toolshed was built at a cost that was so low in materials (the labor, Jock thought, was correspondingly high) we felt it just as well not to ask Kiarie where he had acquired the stone, cement, and sheets of corrugated iron. We wondered what color paint he would bring to finish the job and hoped that he would have the good taste to steal a color we liked.

Once when he was putting in a cement walk for us we came home from town and he was nowhere to be found. It turned out that McDonnell, our younger son, was driving a visiting friend of his to see the Ngong Hills, and Kiarie, who had to know where everyone was going and why, asked if he could ride along too. Thus, in effect, we were paying him to have a picnic lunch overlooking the picturesque Rift Valley from the hills. Somehow it always made us smile—he would not lie about where he had been, and we understood that he simply could not resist the opportunity to learn about anything and everything. (Or perhaps there's some of the "If you like someone, no matter what they do it's all right, and if you don't like them whatever they do is wrong" in there, too.)

Another time Kiarie worked as a nightwatchman for us when we were away and he caught a burglar. I don't know if I would risk my neck tackling a burglar armed with a *panga* for only two dollars a night. He seemed quite fearless. Once when he was topping some tall trees so that we could see the view, I had to close my eyes—it made the palms of my hands sweat to watch him waving and swaying forty feet above the ground with no safety belt. He was having a wonderful time, though, swinging back and forth in the wind high above us and laughing his head off.

On one of our evening walks Jock and I noticed a large fresh hole around a tree in the forest. Upon close examination we saw it had been dug by people, not animals—the pickax marks were very clear and the roots of the tree had been exposed and many of them cut away. Who would come into the forest and dig such a big hole and why? We asked many people, including Kiptanui and Tito, but no one had any idea. The next time Kiarie arrived we showed him, and of course he knew the answer immediately. The roots of this extremely rare tree, he told us, were used in various witchcraft ceremonies and could also be brewed into a kind of tea which gives one *nguvu* (strength).

When Randy Paar came to stay she brought me one of the first mood rings and I slipped it onto Kiarie's finger without telling him about its magic properties. A few minutes later there were cries of delight as the thing changed color and then changed again. "What a wonderful thing for a witch doctor to own," said Kiarie. "Just think how he could *bembeleza* [persuade—or, in Kiarie's language, con] people." Right there he confirmed how his mind worked. In another place and another time Kiarie would have been the imaginative inventor of snake oil, the founder of some theologically weak but highly profitable evangelical movement, or an irresistible salesman of lightweight anvils.

When we moved to Langata, Kiarie was uninvited but on hand, of course, instructing the removal people how to get the grand piano through the front door, showing us where the fishpond was cracked, explaining how he would mend it . . .

Of course Kiarie knew about giraffe. In an effort to entice Tom, Dick, and Harry to stay around when we first moved in we had tied a mineral-salt block high in a tree where they could lick it—but it was a fruitless effort, because they never found it. We then lodged bunches of lucerne hay in the branches, where it hung until it rotted. We did all the things the giraffe experts told us to, but nothing worked: they continued to come and go as they pleased without sampling our goodies. Kiarie said, "They like sweet-potato tops," and in a few days he arrived with a supply in a large cardboard box strapped to the back of his bicycle. How he knew this we could not imagine, but there was no doubt that the giraffe did indeed enjoy the juicy leaves.

In trying also to entice the wild warthogs to come closer we had put our garbage on the lawn, certain they would rush up to devour it within minutes, but what actually happened was that we had garbage all over the lawn for weeks—it lay in stinking little heaps until Kiarie criticized it and cleared it away in a wheelbarrow.

About this time Peter Beard gave us a copy of his new book, *Longing for Darkness*, which is a lovely photo-pictorial selection of memories about the author Isak Dinesen (*Out of Africa, Seven Gothic Tales*, etc.) as seen through the eyes of her cook, Kamante, who had joined her staff when he was a small boy. Isak Dinesen had often written about Kamante and it was Peter Beard's idea, some years earlier, to find out if he was still alive—for if he was he would be an invaluable link in reconstructing much that happened during the period she lived in Kenya between World War I and World War

159

II. Kiarie, it turned out, was the man who had tracked down Kamante for Peter (he had been helping to build a studio for him and had overheard that the search was on for Kamante). To digress for a moment (you will have noticed that we hardly ever permit ourselves a digression), we became friends with Kamante for an odd reason. When Isak Dinesen left Kenya before World War II she gave some of her furniture to Jock's mother. Peter was very excited when we told him, but Jock's mother was dead and although Jock had inherited the furniture there was no way he could *prove* to anyone else that certain pieces had belonged to Isak Dinesen. Then we realized that Kamante might be able to remember, so we pointed it all out to Peter in advance (so that he could be positive that we weren't just ratholing him by simply agreeing with Kamante whatever he might identify), and then we brought Kamante in, and he picked out every single piece independently without a mistake—after a gap of forty years without having seen it!

Remembering Kiarie's involvement in the Kamante saga, I showed Peter's book to him. Although he was unable to read he immediately recognized faces in many of the old photographs and pointed out personalities, tribal chiefs, and others whom he remembered from his childhood. It was always fun showing Kiarie things like this, because he got such pleasure from it and often had interesting little footnotes to add. He was enthusiastic about everything.

So Jock and I did not have to wonder very long about who would build a giraffe boma on short notice. Neither of us had any real idea what was needed. How strong were young giraffe, how much room did they need, and would they like an enclosed area with a roof or something that was open to the skies? Of course Kiarie claimed to know all the answers, having once done some contract work for an animal trapper, and we left it to him while we went off to collect Daisy. A week later, when we returned with her, there, tacked onto one end of the stables, stood the funniest-looking structure we'd ever seen—like an outhouse for a giant. But even if it wouldn't serve as a blueprint for an architect's manual it has nevertheless proved highly acceptable to Daisy.

When the time came to build a new house for the new giraffe we were going to capture, we hoped Kiarie would come around. We also wanted him to enlarge Daisy's house—upward, that is; we were going to raise the roof. (Terrible pun.) We learned upon our return from Malindi that while we had been there Kiarie had come looking for us, but unfortunately we had forgotten to mention to anybody that we wanted him for a job.

Two days later a friend of his, a housepainter, rode in on his bicycle to tell us that Kiarie had hanged himself. He had been unable to find work in the ever-increasing situation of unemployment around Nairobi.

Jock and I both cried.

What a waste—if ever there was a bright man, an agile mind, a positive personality with seemingly endless optimism, it was Kiarie. It was truly heartbreaking to imagine the degree of desperation he must have felt to take his own life. Had he been knocked off his bicycle by a truck, or had one of his doubtful edifices collapsed on him, it would have been dreadful, of course, but not as poignant as this; or had he been a neurotic or a depressed person, his death might have been easier to accept as the ultimate conclusion of defeat in life. Instead it seemed that here was a basically happy man with a great potential, who, finding himself unable to get sufficient work to feed himself and his family, had the intelligence to realize the futility of his existence. His suicide brought the plight of many Africans much closer to us (why does one always need such experiences to bring about true realization?) and his act seems in a way an indictment of the pressures brought to Africa by civilization.

Since then hardly a day has passed when I have not thought about Kiarie. I wish, too, that we could have read these pages about himself to him. How he would have loved them.

Even though Marlon had been kicked by Daisy upon arrival at Langata when he had staggered into the boma like a drunk, he was nevertheless still overjoyed to see one of the clan. Daisy was not.

We put him into his house immediately, but he barely investigated it, he was so preoccupied with Daisy, who snubbed him. After an hour or so of his following her every move and trying to get out to her, she came over and sniffed him through the slats. Then she walked away as if never to speak to him again. We decided that in the morning when she was used to the idea of his being there we'd let them into the boma together and their great friendship could begin.

The next morning when we opened his door Marlon skipped out and rushed up to her ecstatically, for all his instincts told him that the rather larger Daisy, though not as tall as his mother, would surely be a source of milk—the proper kind, not that imitation stuff from an aluminum pan. Daisy kicked him and walked away. But because of his very positive outlook he kept trying to touch her, despite her kicks and her turning away.

161

Daisy, we recalled, had ignored Tom, Dick, and Harry when they had come to greet her the first few times, and we understood that she might similarly be ignoring Marlon, but we had not anticipated the hostility. Finally we let Daisy out of the boma into the garden—she was most relieved to get away from that nuisance—but Marlon paced up and down inside the fence, as he was to do for days to come, looking at Daisy on the lawn and trying to get to her. It was entirely a one-sided arrangement and Daisy couldn't have cared less, being under no illusion about Marlon's ability to contribute to *her* well-being. She ignored the kid.

At feeding times Daisy stuck to her established routine of eying the preparation of warm milk through a hole high in the wall of the tackroom next door which allowed her to supervise what was going on inside. Marlon, a prisoner in his house for his own safety from supper time until after breakfast each morning, knew it was mealtime, too, but the smell of milk only reinforced what he had learned from his mother, viz. that larger giraffe feed smaller giraffe. Thus when we held the pan out for him and made encouraging noises he would try pathetically, and with more determination than ever, to

162

get to Daisy, as if it were she who was exerting all this loving care for his benefit.

After four days of this, Marlon had hardly drunk at all and was only toying with the right leaves tied on to the wrong trees. Jock and I knew that somehow we had to convince Marlon that we were a better bet than Daisy, and I started spending up to five and six hours a day in his pen with him while Daisy was wandering around in the garden. Whenever she was out of sight Marlon would pay some attention to me. He began by sucking my thumb and having his neck stroked at the same time, but Daisy had only to come into view a hundred yards away for a few seconds to break the spell and have him pacing up and down near the fence. I started taking my typewriter down to Marlon's boma and sitting in there with him, and after a week of this Marlon would accept the occasional pint of milk from the pan which I held under his nose, but he was not eating or drinking on any regular basis. The disadvantage of leaving the milk and allowing him to help himself was that there was no way of keeping it constantly warm, and cold milk, we were told, was a sure way to trigger a stomach upset. In the end, because we were afraid that he would starve himself to death, we did leave the milk and quickly found that Marlon was not only a problem drinker but a secret drinker as well. However carefully we hid and spied on him or asked Tito and the others to do the same, we could never actually catch him in the act of tippling. We had to accept the fact that we had a young closet drinker on our hands—until one day we found out that it was Daisy who was syphoning it off through the railings. I continued to offer him warm milk three or four times a day, but other than a halfhearted sip every now and then he had no interest in it.

The love-hate relationship between the two twiga deepened on both sides each day. Marlon's ogling of Daisy continued through the railings and she continued to ignore him, which resulted in him imposing a near-starvation diet on himself, if not quite a full-scale Gandhi-style hunger strike.

We were operating a cumbersome system of ensuring that Marlon and Daisy were never in the boma at the same time. In the mornings this was fairly easy, since we would feed them both in their own houses, release Daisy, and close the boma gate so that she could not get back in again. Then we would let Marlon out of his house within the boma and he had the exclusive run of it all day until evening feeding time, when we tried to lure him back in. Had he been anx-

ious to get at the milk this would have presented no problem, because all I would have had to do was walk into his house and he would have followed me, but with his fasting there was no incentive other than carrots, and he would forgo even them to get at Daisy. There was no other way which we could think of to lure him in and there was certainly no way to drive him in. Unlike a horse, or a dog, or even a cow, a wild animal cannot just have a rope put on it and be dragged around. With weeks of effort we could probably have trained Daisy and Marlon to wear a head collar, but disciplining wild creatures is not easy—and it was not our objective. They were to be released, not put into a circus.

About this time a man who belonged to the Spanish school of riding and who had trained performing horses (a typical kind of person to live in Kenya) heard about Daisy and sent a message that he would like to train her to be ridden. I must say it matched our Walter Mitty fantasies of fitting her up with a saddle and some kind of bridle and getting Rick to freak out everybody at the polo ground—or, better still, to turn up at one of the meets of the local hunt which still does its thing, pink coats, master of hounds, stirrup cups, and all. It's a great fantasy and endlessly tempting, and I seriously believe that it could be done. After all, Dr. Dolittle was undoubtedly seen aboard a giraffe in the film of the same name, and Tarzan sat astride one in an old movie, but whether they were heavily drugged (Dr. Dolittle and Tarzan, that is) in order to obtain the footage is not clear. Or maybe the giraffe they used was Cha Cha Cha Morales . . .

Seriously, though, on principle we wouldn't attempt that kind of thing, because we are busy *not* making pets out of Daisy and Marlon, whatever you may think. Nor do we want them to become famous film stars like Lassie—we don't want people rushing up to them and asking "May I have your autogiraffe?" Rutherfurd agreed and said, "That's not what they're meant to do." They will be taught no tricks, will not be made to do cute little things, will not be required to obey, and are free to do whatever they want—especially since we have absolutely no control over them anyway.

Speaking of autographs and film stars reminds me of something silly that occurred soon after we got Marlon. It just happens that on our last visit to the States we had a five-hour lunch with the real Marlon (Brando). If it interests you, he is incredibly well versed in environmental subjects, population growths, global food shortages, feeding mankind from the sea, and much more along those lines.

There were five of us in a private home and never once did the conversation even brush for a second on the topic of movies or acting. There was a possibility that Marlon might come to Kenya to look at a scheme to restore land reduced to desert by cattle and goats through the reintroduction of the wild animals who lived there in the first place, and we had mentioned this to some friends. Thus, when word got out that "Marlon" had arrived at the Leslie-Melvilles', we were subjected to surprise visits by various females who turned up coyly on the pretext of coming to say hello to Daisy. Their disappointment was offset only by the fact that *our* Marlon, too, is so adorable.

But to get back to the boma problems, we were forced to allow about an hour every evening to get Marlon locked up in his house so that Daisy could come into the boma for her supper and for the night. True, it would have been easy to feed Daisy outside, or anywhere, since she would have followed her milk pan into the center of Nairobi during rush hour if we wanted, but we felt that for longer-term reasons of making her feel secure she should keep on being fed in her house and should sleep there, too.

One evening we conned Marlon into the upper end of the boma and tried to blockade him there with a long steel pipe in order to keep him from running out when we opened the gate at the lower end to let Daisy in. After he was trapped in the upper part and Daisy came skipping merrily in and headed for her house—ignoring Marlon, of course—he ran to her just as if there were no length of pipe across his path at all. My God, I thought, he's going right into it and will break all four legs. Flat out he ran, and at the last minute he merely ducked under the rail—it was no obstacle at all. He got up to Daisy and tried to suckle her and she kicked him badly. Daisy was nearly twice his size in terms of weight and about a third again as tall.

You can see what a rotten situation it was—much worse than before, when Daisy, if not ecstatic alone, was at least contented. Now she had a minus in her life, Marlon, who irritated her, and he, poor little chap, who had been such a good starter, was miserable and frustrated and wouldn't eat.

After a full week of my concentrating love on Marlon, and his concentrating love on Daisy, quite suddenly, for no reason that we could discern he thrust his nose all the way into the milk pan which I was holding and sucked the milk down like a child with an ice

166

cream soda. He must have said to himself, "Ah, to hell with Daisy, I'll pick the ugly one—at least she loves me." And when he finished his milk, he looked down and kissed me in the eye.

He continued to watch Daisy, but now it was more out of curiosity than from any imagined need. Daisy didn't notice the change in him any more than she had noticed being the object of so much long-distance adoration by him since his arrival. Having transferred his love to me, he became overly affectionate—sucking my thumb for long periods of time, rubbing his face against mine, eating my buttons, chewing my hair, my clothes, my belt. We'd sit touching, then we'd stand together side by side, just Marlon and I, and watch Daisy and Shirley Brown and Tito and the warthogs. Then he'd rub his neck across my back and kiss me, and rub his neck across my back again. Then he'd get mad because I didn't know how to rub my

neck on him in the proper giraffe fashion, but he loved me anyway, dummy that I am—and funny-looking too.

If it weren't such a cliché, I'd say love conquered all.

I'm almost embarrassed to tell you this, but, well—we eat leaves together. At least I pretend to because he doesn't like to eat alone. It reminds me of when I used to try to get my kids to eat some unbearable slop by going "Yum-yum uuuummmm goood," and pretending to have some myself; and now I'm eating leaves. But it doesn't work any better with Marlon than it did with the kids. He reacts the same way: thinks I'm telling him the truth, tries the new kind of leaf, then promptly spits it out and looks me with distaste—"Liar."

Now that Marlon had imprinted on me instead of Daisy we thought maybe he'd stop trying to suckle her, since he had me and my thumb. Jock and I talked about trying again to let him join Daisy in the boma but decided that there should be a period of consolidation to make absolutely sure that Marlon knew we were his sole meal ticket; there was no point in risking any backsliding by allowing him access to her prematurely.

When he had been taking food from us eagerly for more than two weeks and apparently ignoring Daisy we decided to try it. After their breakfast one morning when they were both presumably full and contented, we didn't open the gate for Daisy to go into the garden as usual, but simply let Marlon out of his house into the boma, where Daisy was munching leaves. We had no idea whether there would be an immediate set-to of some kind or whether they would ignore each other.

Marlon bounced out of his doorway in his usual cocky early-morning fashion, and pulled up when he saw Daisy. She, sensing that something unusual was going on, turned around and looked at him for about fifteen seconds. Then they walked towards each other in the open and touched noses. Immediately after this, stylized like ballet dancers, they arched their necks and placed their foreheads together, and they stood that way for maybe ten seconds. Then Daisy swung her head high in the air, turned, and kicked Marlon with her hind legs, but in a very halfhearted manner as if to establish pecking order before returning to her branch. Marlon walked over to me and I kissed him and rubbed his mane and gave him a

carrot (which he now loved) to prove to him I was a better mother than crazy Daisy. Sensing that goodies were being dished out, Daisy came over, too, and reached for a carrot and at the same time gave a gentle front-footed side swipe at Marlon, who backed off a pace or two.

We watched for about half an hour, during most of which time they chewed leaves or took carrots from me independently and seemed to ignore each other. Then Marlon made his way down to the far end of the boma and stood there, minding his own business. All of a sudden Daisy looked at him with a beady eye and charged the luckless little fellow, crashing into him with a thud which very nearly knocked him off his feet. She followed through, kicking at him in earnest and forcing him back towards the far fence. Then, as suddenly as she had started, she stopped and walked over to help herself to some more leaves.

Jock and I were both a little shocked at the vehemence of Daisy's sudden attack and decided that that was enough for one day. Had it come immediately following their confrontation it might have been more understandable, but it happened just at the moment when we were starting to relax and to congratulate ourselves that we had timed their meeting very well. However, if Daisy's attack was a minus, the plus was that Marlon had definitely ceased to regard Daisy as any kind of mother figure.

We decided that we had better let Daisy out. Before doing this we had to get Marlon back into his own house, or into Daisy's, so that he wouldn't dash out of the boma gate along with her. It was like playing boatman, fox, and chicken. The incident of a few minutes earlier had disturbed Marlon's equilibrium, and try as we might we could not persuade him to go into his house. He and Daisy were still in the boma together, and we grew more and more apprehensive that she might attempt another attack and that if she did she might even get Marlon down on the ground, where she could trample him severely. After about twenty minutes of rattling pans and pretending to offer milk, all of which got Daisy into a high state of excitement but had no effect at all on the chastened Marlon, we did succeed in luring him into Daisy's house. Tito nipped through the railings and closed the door behind him.

Although Marlon had been wandering in and out of her house every day for the past two weeks while she was outside the boma, now evidently being trapped in her territory with her nearby somehow frightened him and he panicked and tried to get out, lunging at

170

the railings in his efforts to escape. Quickly we opened the boma gate, rushed Daisy out, and locked the boma again so that we could spring Marlon from his temporary prison which was having such a bad effect on him. He bounded out and, in what we had by then come to regard as typical giraffe fashion, was restored from near-hysteria to serenity within a matter of seconds.

We decided to defer another meeting in the boma until he and Daisy had had two or three more weeks to get really bored with each other through the railings. Poor little Marlon—he was so sweet and gentle and he had done nothing at all to attract the ire of Daisy. His behavior was impeccable, he had been polite and shy and not in the least precocious.

During lunch we concluded that perhaps Daisy was jealous of Marlon. Although Jock was still giving her her milk and I would go up to her a few times a day with some carrots, I had been concentrating almost solely on Marlon, spending my time with him, not her. We also wondered if we had made the right decision in acquiring Marlon. In anthropomorphic fashion we had allowed ourselves to be seduced by the conviction that Daisy would need a companion of her own age and would suffer pangs of loneliness without someone to play with. Tom, Dick, and Harry and the rest of the gang were so much older that she would have little in common with them. Furthermore, like hopeful grandparents, we had speculated about Daisy's children by Marlon when they grow up in three or four years. If all went well, we could expect a little Rothschild fifteen months after that, or in other words when Daisy was five. (Their baby would be six feet tall when born and would weigh at least 125 pounds.)

Now, however, it seemed that the only results of bringing Marlon to Langata were that he had been badly upset for a couple of weeks imagining Daisy was his mother, and that Daisy, in turn, wanted nothing to do with him, even when he wasn't annoying her. Her jealousy was now understandable in retrospect—after all, she had had undivided attention for several months and perhaps had grown to relish being an only child. But was this line of thinking anthropomorphic, too? Perhaps giraffe simply did not need other giraffe, that's what the book said, except in the sense of a large loose herd—and maybe they didn't need them at all. How would one know? Has anyone yet done a giraffe Rorschach test?

Would Daisy ever have any need of Marlon, and in the years ahead would they provide companionship for each other or simply irritation and jealousy? If the latter were the case, would that be fair to Daisy? She had seemed happier before. Should we send Marlon—perish the thought—to the orphanage? Or, short of such a drastic step, should we build Marlon a little complex of his own on the far side of the property, well out of sight of Daisy's boma, and hope for the best when they were both running free?

Jock told me that probably, as is the way with most animals that are exposed to one another over a long period, even across the boundary of species, a kind of companionship *would* develop between Daisy and Marlon, so we decided to carry on as before for a few more weeks and then try again. He went on to tell me that Konrad Lorenz, the Nobel Prize–winning animal behaviorist, has observed a relationship that developed between a lone fish and a lone swan. It ended in tragedy with a fisherman catching the fish and the death of the swan within a week through pining. Similarly he has written of an old horse turned out to pasture by itself in a field which it shared with a crippled wild partridge that was unable to fly. The two became inseparable companions and for years were never more than a few yards apart. Recently, too, in the Cincinnati zoo we saw a baby rhino and a sheep sharing the same room. The keeper told us that they had had to remove the rhino from its mother because she was clumsy and had injured it by treading on it and bumping into it. The sheep, which had been living alone was put in with the baby and the two now adored and needed each other, baaing and crying pathetically if ever they were separated. Jock also told me about a polo pony belonging to his stepfather which preferred the company of a goat to other horses' to the extent that the goat had to travel with it around the country to various polo tournaments, sharing the horse box and the stall at all times.

I glared at him. "You're telling me *now*—after all we've been through to capture Marlon and bring him here—that we could have got Daisy a goat or a crippled partridge *instead?*"

172

8

Please Don't Eat
the Daisy

Who's ever heard of anyone who doesn't like a giraffe? We have. The man who manages Lewa Downs, Rutherfurd's friend Ken McBride, loathes them. When he saw us coming to catch Daisy he said, "Can't you take the whole lot away?" It is understandable why he doesn't like them—they have knocked down his fences and trampled crops grown for fodder and made it hard for him to run a profitable ranch for David Craig.

And for the same understandable reasons the many African families buying Lewa Downs will poach every last Rothschild.

"Giraffe make good eating too," said Ken with a leer, rubbing it in, and we winced as we envisioned him tucking into a Daisy steak. Yet, were we saving calves, we would no doubt wince at people eating veal parmigiana. It's all conditioning.

Not long ago in Ethiopia as we walked by a lake, Jock and I

noticed that the birds on the shore didn't make any attempt to get out of our way, let alone to fly off. "What's wrong with your birds?" I asked an Ethiopian friend who was with us.

"Nothing is wrong with our birds," he replied patiently. "It is *your* birds which are afraid. Here in Ethiopia we have a commandment, 'Thou shalt not eat webfooted birds.' Therefore they are not hunted, are not afraid and don't fly away."

I am trying to spread a new commandment around Kenya, "Thou shalt not eat cloven-hoofed giraffe." And above all, "Please don't eat the Daisy."

Yet, like sex, it's probably all in the mind. A giraffe is unbelievably beautiful, it has liquid eyes and film-star lashes, it is gentle and graceful and it doesn't bother anyone. A crocodile is equally a creature of the African wild. It is not attractive to look at, having an inbuilt reptilian capacity to cause revulsion in man, and its meat is seldom consumed by humans (though the Turkana people at Lake Rudolph will sometimes eat them). We would probably pay very little attention if someone told us he had belted a croc or two, yet were we logical and absolute in our wishes to see African wildlife survive we should be far more concerned over the shooting of crocodile because they are a faster dwindling species, than over the killing of giraffe. (Leaving aside for a moment the fact that there are so few *Rothschild* giraffe.)

Jane Goodall's films have improved the sad image of the habitually vilified hyena, but it is a fact about wildlife lovers that most of them (us) are more selective than we should be and tend to go overboard for the preservation of the cuddly, the beautiful, and the magnificent, rather than for the nasties and the heavies of the animal world. Actually I am exaggerating. The more serious among the conservationists passed through this barrier long ago and see in their minds a picture of perfect eco-balance in which every species has its place. The typical amateur enthusiast, however, falls easily into the trap in which we sometimes find ourselves as well, of being mainly concerned with the adorables. Speaking of which (horrifying story coming up), there are a couple of snake parks at Malindi, one of which is not as concerned about the sensibilities of its visitors as the other. Snakes, as you may know, will not eat anything they have not killed themselves and thus have to be fed live chicks, mice, frogs, and so on. I've watched only once, and it's not a spectacle I wish to see again. Freshly hatched little yellow chicks were on the menu that day, and they were dropped into the glass-fronted boxes containing the snakes. Surprisingly, nothing happened at first and the little things hopped about peeping pathetically, even jumping onto the backs of the deadly still snakes. Then suddenly a snake struck—so fast you could hardly see—and was still again. Within a minute the chick started to stagger, and its peep grew weaker until it rolled over, twitching. Then the snake opened its mouth, and over about fifteen minutes it enveloped the chick, distending its jaws and bulging out in the process. Anyhow, when supplies of chicks and mice run low, the owners of the insensitive snake park dash off to the surrounding African villages and buy up as many tiny *puppies* as they can to feed live to the snakes.

175

You will probably agree that no American would eat Flipper, yet in this same sentence I can truthfully write that over one hundred thousand porpoises are killed each year by Americans when they are caught in the nets of fishermen providing you with light meat tuna. You see, I think part of the trouble is that it *isn't* all in the mind, because people don't know about these things, and if they did I don't believe they would be cruel enough to allow them to go on happening. I didn't know about the porpoises in the nets, but when I learned about it I returned my can of tuna fish to the A & P—and I love tuna fish. But even more I love the thought of porpoises not crying and hollering as they die. "Would you kill Flipper for a tuna-fish sandwich?" is a good sign. And I have enough faith in human beings being human to bet that if they knew and understood the whole picture, they would stop it. Even if they had to give up light meat tuna fish for a while.

It's the same with fur coats. I believe, really believe, that if people knew how hideously the animals died, they wouldn't wear fur coats. When you buy a fur coat the salesperson doesn't tell you how the foxes or lynx or whatever are trapped in steeljaw traps, which is equivalent to our getting our hand caught in a car door, only worse because *we* can get it out. They struggle for days and nights and sometimes weeks, suffering unimaginable pain, thirst, cold and hunger. More than 25 million wild animals are trapped or snared every year for the fur trade! The furriers know—they're the bad guys—but I really don't think people who buy fur coats are aware of the torture and the horror.

Do you think anyone who knew what is happening to the baby seals could wear a coat made from their fur? Baby seals, who respond to cuddling by wrapping their flippers around your fingers, are born early every March in Canada, and four days later their fur turns pure white and stays that way for about two weeks only. It is during this time that Canadian and Norwegian hunters descend on the seal while they are nursing and club and beat the babies to death while the terrified mothers stand by watching. Observers have described wails of anguish from the bewildered mothers as they watch their babies being clubbed and skinned.

How about whales? The largest mammals that have ever lived, and also among the most intelligent, whales have been around for a long time, and have been known to man for a long time, too, as frequent references to them in the Bible will testify. A whale dies every twelve minutes—a horrible agonizing death. Every twelve minutes. Over one hundred whales are harpooned each day, their meat made into dog food and cat food, mostly, and the oil is used in paint and for car transmissions—for which there are many, often cheaper, substitutes available.

Whales are very affectionate and won't desert their wounded. Whalers take advantage of this by harpooning a baby and towing it into the whaling station, thereby luring its mother and sometimes the whole family for butchering too.

Yet whales are decent to man. People photographing them and diving among them report the effort whales make to *avoid* hurting man. Whales are more humane than humans.

Dr. George Small observes in his book, *The Blue Whale*,

> The tragedy of the blue whale is in the reflection of an even greater one, that of man himself. What is the nature of a species that knowingly and without good reason exterminates another? When will man learn that he is but one form of life among countless thousands, each of which is in some way related to and dependent on all others? How long will man persist in the belief that he is the master of the Earth rather than one of its guests?

But what can *you* do? you ask. You can't go to Canada and club the men who club the seals; you can't go to Japan and Russia, the worst of the whale-killing countries by far, and stop them. No, you can't, but there are things you *can* do. Often if people know what to do they are prepared to do it. I believe that it is not only the lack of knowledge about these things, but the lack of knowing what to *do* about these things that causes us to allow such atrocities to continue.

Anyone who has just read this last page can no longer plead innocence.

So what can you do? Maybe you can't go to Washington to lobby, but there are excellent organizations which do just that, and get results. (Americans can no longer import whale products, for example, though the British still can.) You can contribute to such an organization—even a small amount helps. You can boycott Japanese and Russian goods, you can refrain from buying zebra-skin rugs, or jewelry made out of ivory or tortoise shell, and you can make others aware by talking about it. Lewis Regenstein's book, *The Politics of Extinction*, is excellent on this subject. That's what we need: a few more Ralph Naders of the animal world.

What of hunting? If it is carefully controlled, is used to limit possibly harmful excesses of certain animals in a given area, and if heavy licensing fees are levied from hunters and the money plowed back into conservation, is it not helpful? This *can* be true, and we have said it ourselves, but the fact is that in Africa today wherever hunting is legal a vast parallel abuse of the law also goes on. Some of the very officials who issue the permits and are supposed to control hunting are at the same time shooting illicitly for profit themselves, or are accepting bribes to give licenses to others who want to get rich from ivory and skins. Were there a total ban on hunting any shot ringing out in the wilds would advertise the presence of a criminal, any attempt to sell a horn or tusk would result in prosecution. Of course a ban on licensed hunting will not end poaching, but it can help. And such a ban has now been imposed in Kenya.

Hunters bother me on another level, too. I just can't understand anyone who not only kills, but *enjoys* killing. A "sport"? What's the sport of a man in a camouflage suit creeping up on an elephant or a zebra giraffe which just stands there and looks at him while he pulls the trigger?

What about bird shooting? "Skill's the thing there," the "sportsmen" tell us. But if so, why not shoot at targets, at clay pigeons? No, the killing is the pleasure—which I find appalling—yet there are still many people who think it respectable to kill not only birds, but lion and leopard and antelope too.

For those who will tell me that hunting is a wonderful thing to do with one's son—comradeship, outdoorsmanship—all I can say is I don't see what's so great about teaching your son to enjoy killing, or inflicting pain with indifference, and teaching him to be unfeeling about suffering. Go on a photographic safari with him. All the excitement of hunting is there—sometimes even more in getting close to an elephant while unarmed—and the animals live.

What right have we to eliminate another species? For our pleasure, which is hunting? For our vanity, which is fashion? For our commerce, which is killing an elephant for its ivory, a giraffe for the hair from its tail?

I understand people's having bought elephant-hair bracelets and giraffe-hair bracelets. I bought them myself years ago because I didn't know. But do you have to wait till you see, as Jock and I have seen, a giraffe lying down, dying a slow and painful death from a poacher's poisoned arrow in its stomach before you stop buying giraffe-hair bracelets?

Of course the poacher is wrong, but I have no trouble understanding him. I can understand that he doesn't understand—he is usually a simple peasant trying to make a few cents to feed his family. He probably can't read, and he has no concept of the larger-scale destruction in which he is involved. He *can* plead innocence, but you and I cannot, and we are the ones who are responsible and who create the market if we buy the goods. The middle man who pays the poacher almost nothing, and who sells to us marked up a thousand percent or more is the knowing venal villain of the tragedy, the ultimate pariah.

In Saks Jock and I have demanded to see the buyer because they were offering a colobus monkey-skin rug for sale. In Bloomingdale's we saw the buyer, too, about zebra skin rugs—little brownish zebra skins which meant they were babies. We have written to the presidents of the stores about these things, threatening to close our charge accounts and to persuade our friends to do likewise; and to be fair, we have had good responses pleading ignorance and promising not to transgress in future. You see, it does work. In New York I went into Nikon House at Fifty-second Street and Madison Avenue and asked if many people were boycotting Japanese cameras because of the whales. We can all make others aware.

Since you started reading this section another whale has been killed.

Is killing of wild animals ever justified? The answer is yes. Occasionally, and after proper consideration, it may be necessary. For instance, Tsavo Park in Kenya supported about thirty thousand elephant, and for thousands of years they had been living happily in and around their Tsavo land of plenty, wandering out of the eight-thousand square-mile area (the size of New Jersey) from time to time during a drought in order to seek food elsewhere. Then, with modern medicine, the incredible human population explosion began in Kenya. (Next to Algeria we have the fastest rate of population growth in the world—an ominous and terrifying thought.) And as more and more humans encroach on more and more land the animals are constantly being pushed back and encircled, denied their migration routes, barred from emergency supplies of food. Tsavo is no exception, and the elephant could no longer move out of their territory in lean times, because man wouldn't let them. Thus the great beasts were confined, and fifteen years back the effect started to be seen as too many of them tried to live off too little vegetation.

Being so large, elephant need to consume huge amounts of food to keep themselves going; for sixteen hours out of each twenty-four these vegetarians work at filling their stomachs from the trees and bushes around them. Soon there was little left in Tsavo in the way of their usual food and they had pushed over most of the trees to get at the green branches out of reach, so they started to eat the grass, which is also quite acceptable fodder for them. Now the whole environment was being destroyed, not just for the elephant themselves but also for the antelope who could no longer find enough grazing and for the lion who could no longer find sufficient antelope.

An ecologist was called in to give his opinion on the devastation, and he recommended culling three thousand elephant. Doesn't that sound terrible? Kill three thousand elephant? Yes, he agreed, it did sound terrible, but the alternative, he pointed out, was worse. The way to do it, he explained, would be to get professional hunters who knew what they were about, to shoot out entire families at a time so that there would be no grieving elephant. The meat could readily be used in a protein-starved country and the valuable ivory could be sold legally to help pay for the conservation of the park and the other animals. With the reduced load of elephant the environment stood a chance of righting itself and returning to normal.

But pressure was too strong against him and nobody followed his recommendations—in fact, he left the country. Between five- and ten-thousand elephant starved to death in the following years, a fate far worse than being shot, and the remaining ones were staggering around like half-starved zombies, having reduced their territory practically to desert—a desert strewn with the bleached bones of dead elephant, unsuitable now for the other animals as well. Unhappily the problem was greatly worsened by the failure of the seasonal rains for several years after that, and heaven knows how low the elephant population of Tsavo has now sunk because man could not bring himself to act in their interests in time. Tsavo is still a terrible sight and enough to prove to us, at any rate, that man, having caused the imbalance, must now do his best to scientifically rectify the situation. Either the people have to go or the animals have to go, and since I doubt if everyone would agree to it being people, then culling is occasionally the only answer.

Proof that it works was demonstrated on the Kazinga Channel in Western Uganda some years ago where there was a population explosion of hippo who had nowhere else to move (human settlement all around), and who were well on the way to destroying their habitat as the elephants did in Tsavo. In a matter of months the numbers of hippo were expertly halved by scientists and professionals shooting them, and the meat sold to needy villagers. Within a year or two the vegetation had returned to the water's edge and the place became a thriving balanced game area once more.

Our belief in this kind of intervention from time to time makes Jock and me "conservationists" instead of "preservationists." I didn't even know there was a difference, but it seems that the leave-it-to-nature camp are the preservationists and are appalled by what they regard as callous interference by those who would crop or control surplus wild-animal populations. Conservationists, on the other hand, maintain that you cannot always leave to nature that which is no longer a natural situation.

Another justification for killing an animal would be when one is wounded or badly injured. Recently we hit an antelope and broke its back when it ran in front of the car. Jock got out and slit its throat at once. You shouldn't let an animal suffer and die slowly in agony.

In other words we are not against death. (Actually I am—very much against it—but I haven't yet figured out how to avoid it.) If we were against all killing of animals we would not wear leather shoes and gloves, eat hamburgers, and wear suede jackets, all of which we do.

Man, it seems to me, has always utilized the living protein around him in one form or another, and provided he does so with due regard to the continuation of those animals from which he benefits, and provided he dispatches them with the utmost humanity I guess we are in no position to be too critical.

Many people strongly oppose this and believe that man should not kill other living creatures in order to benefit therefrom. Animal lovers in this sense are true vegetarians who will not even eat to-mato aspic because hoofs are used in the manufacture of gelatin, and who will buy no cosmetics or soaps or anything else containing animal fat. These people protect all living creatures—snakes, mos-quitoes, and cockroaches, as well as whales and baby seals and gi-raffe and lion cubs. In short, they live out what they proclaim, and it is an attractive and compelling notion. But it does seem to me that there is a halfway position on the subject, and that, much as we hate killing anything, the greater good is surely to have dead mos-quitoes and rats rather than dead people from malaria and bubonic plague, and to control the population of animals when necessary to save them from themselves. But meanwhile we will continue to put spiders out of windows instead of killing them and will exert our-selves to the utmost to ensure that sheep, giraffe, Angus cattle, pen-guins, aardvarks—everything—do not become endangered species.

All are agreed, however—the sentimental preservationists and the pragmatic conservators—that poaching on the scale that is happening in East Africa is a terrible threat.

But why should the animals here be safeguarded at all? So that a fraction of one percent of the elite of the world can derive enjoyment by coming to East Africa on safari to look at them? That is not the question. The animals provide an amazing self-regenerating natural resource (through tourism) from which the country and the poor people here can continue forever to make a great deal of money with hardly any effort—if things are handled properly. Moreover, we have a priceless and irreplaceable heritage to maintain on behalf of mankind, who in ignorance and greed has destroyed so much in the world already. We are about to choose, once and for all, if we are going to destroy these things of beauty, which like our van Goghs and Michelangelos, are irreplaceable. Are we not to share the planet with other animals and trees and birds, but to live in a chemical plastic world devoid of wonder?

Who will control the greed of the gross get-rich-quick individuals who threaten to wipe it all out first? *That* is the only real question.

A friend of ours, Chryssee Martin, was an honorary park warden and worked at the Animal Orphanage in Nairobi Game Park every Sunday. We dropped in to see how she was and how things were going at the orphanage, and were delighted to see it filled with African families by the busload who were there learning about the game, their priceless heritage which many of them had probably never had the opportunity to see before. (Soon, they too will not be able to plead innocence about the slaughter going on in their country.)

Chryssee was going from enclosure to enclosure giving a running commentary to the crowd, explaining that the leopard cubs' mother had been poached and that the rhino was there for the same reason, and that the chimpanzee had come from western Uganda, and so on. She could go in with most of the animals, and as she fed and stroked them she would explain to the people about their habits and background and distribution. Finally she came to an enclosure containing a bear. Before she had time to tell them that it had been with a traveling Indian circus and that the SPCA had forcibly confiscated it because the circus people were mistreating it, a nicely dressed African, obviously educated since he spoke English so well, pointed to the bear and asked, "What is that?" I was astonished that anyone in the world wouldn't know what a bear was. I just assumed that everyone had read "Goldilocks and the Three Bears" or had seen a teddy bear, or at least knew there were such animals as bears and roughly what they looked like.

Once again, I was judging other people by my standards, not theirs. I didn't know what an aardwolf was until the other day. We were staying with the Craigs, and David had taken us out in his Hemingway vehicle looking for game at night with a spotlight. I had just seen my first aardvark (ant bear—the villain who makes all those holes in the ground to trap Douglas at Lewa Downs), and then I spotted an animal I didn't recognize. Confused, but hating to appear ignorant, I kept quiet until I could get a closer look, and then I said, "There's a koala bear over there." I was told it was a baby aardwolf, which are very seldom seen and which I had never even heard of. Obviously I knew it couldn't be a koala bear, but I didn't know it was an aardwolf, so what makes me so different from the African who didn't know about the bear?

As a matter of fact it really is hard to get a good look at an aardvark in the wilds. They are so strictly nocturnal and so shy that unless you are deliberately looking for one with a powerful spotlight as we were, and are prepared to devote much time to the search, you will not succeed. The only aardvark I have seen close up is named Emilion and belongs to Alan Root, the renowned wildlife photographer (*The Baobab, Mzima Springs, The Year of the Wildebeest, Hot Air Balloon Over Africa*), and his wife, Joan. It is looked after by a man who is retarded and whose main function in life is to follow Emilion around filling in the holes as he digs them in the garden, and the poor man has found happiness and contentment by being needed and useful. We asked Alan why he had chosen the name Emilion for an ant bear and he got down on one knee like Al Jolson and sang, "Aardvark Emilion miles for one of your smiles, my little Maaaammmmy . . ."

Alan and Joan live on the shore of Lake Naivasha and this enables them to have a pet hippo called Sally, who lives like Daisy and Marlon: she forages for herself and mingles with wild hippos a bit when they come around, but likes to spend most of her time *chez* Root. She too adores, and is adored in return, by the retarded man. It has just occurred to me that perhaps I shouldn't have stressed how fond Daisy and Marlon are of Jock and me. . . .

Wildlife photographers like Simon Trevor (who shot that splendid film *The African Elephant*) and Alan Root expose themselves to considerable risk but on a calculated and not a foolhardy basis.

Even so, things go wrong occasionally. Recently Alan was filming hippos underwater in Mzima Springs when one of them got annoyed and attacked. A hippo can bite a man clean in two as if he were an hors d'oeuvre. This one first took a chomp at Joan, who was helping Alan, and its teeth separated her goggles from her face but left her unscathed—an incredibly close escape. Then it turned upon Alan and grabbed him by the calf of one leg before throwing him out onto the bank. The Flying Doctors got him to Nairobi in time, and for several weeks Alan hovered on the verge of having to have his leg amputated, but the doctors did a terrific job and he now walks normally—all the way back to the hippo.

Dinner parties in Kenya are a common form of entertainment. One seldom goes to restaurants, because most people have a cook and the food is better, and it is cheaper and more pleasant to entertain at home. Nairobi is something of a cultural desert, certainly when compared to Western cities of equivalent size; and the single channel of television, which puts out four hours of Swahili programs a day about planting beans or the effects of soil erosion, interlarded with *Little House on the Prairie* or *Barnaby Jones* (and sometimes *Popeye*), is hardly likely to enslave you as a regular watcher. But the good result of having less television and entertainment available means that the art of conversation is not as lost in Kenya as it seems to be in many places in the world.

Occasionally there are even black-tie dinners. Just before the last one that we were invited to, Jock discovered that he had left his tuxedo in New York. He did a very inventive thing: he took his black blazer with brass buttons and wrapped black masking tape over each button, and no one even noticed. (Try that the next time you're stuck for a tuxedo.) On that particular night one of the guests, a veterinarian, was very late arriving, and when he finally came in, apologizing, he explained he was late because just as he was leaving someone brought a pet python to him because the snake wouldn't eat. (Try that for an excuse next time you're late.) As we always say, "All the world loves a lion cub, but who loves a python?" so we were glad to learn there was someone who did.

That evening Pat Cavendish, who used to have a pet lion, told us that one day her cook had come running to her as she was working at the bottom of the garden and said to come quickly, there was a dead man on the living-room sofa. Pat hurried up to the house and there indeed on her sofa lay a completely strange man with a bald head who appeared to be dead, but who on closer inspection proved to be breathing but unconscious. It turned out that he was visiting the country and didn't know Pat or that she had a lion, but he was to meet a friend who was staying at her house and, arriving early and seeing no one around, had quietly let himself in and sat down on the sofa. The lion, coming silently through an open door, had spotted his bald head from behind and had mistaken it for a football of almost the identical size and color with which it always used to play, so it leaped onto the back of the sofa and grabbed his head with both paws and roared, whereupon the man fainted. It took them nearly an hour to bring him round. Then he left—he wouldn't even stay for tea.

Another time, Pat said, she returned from a shopping trip to Nairobi and failed to see her lion around, so she asked the cook where it was. "Out back with the naked lady," he replied. Fearing that some sexual weirdo was about to make an attempt on her beloved lion's virginity, she rushed out, to find a photographer taking pictures of a nubile blond model and the lion for a *Playboy*-style magazine. A friend of Pat's had mentioned the possibility of the lion's availability for this kind of work, and the photographer had simply turned up and gone ahead without having spoken to Pat about it. I suggested to Jock that he might pose naked with Daisy for *Playgirl*.

What a delightfully nutsy country Kenya is. The place is filled with eccentric individuals doggedly pursuing their own particular lines, quite unaware that there is anything unusual about them at all.

For instance, two days earlier I had come home from town and found a thirty-year-old battered orange motorcycle leaning against a tree near the giraffe boma. I assumed it belonged to one of my son's awful friends and looked around but couldn't see anybody, so I walked into the house. In the living room a very elderly man wearing a Mickey Mouse T-shirt was sitting on the floor surrounded by a thousand pieces of our piano's insides. I am not often at a loss for something to say, but to cover my surprise I asked, "Oh, do you know whose motorcycle that is outside?"

"Yes, it's mine," he answered, "I've just been to Cape Town on it to see my daughter." Cape Town is nearly three thousand miles from Nairobi, and most of the journey is through desolate Africa. I was just wondering whom to call when he introduced himself as Alban Barberton, and it transpired that a mutual friend had heard us asking about a piano tuner (hard to come by in Africa) and had arranged for Alban to come but had forgotten to tell us. Jock and I

185

were so fascinated after talking to him for a few minutes that we asked him to dinner that night along with a piano-playing friend. Alban brought his violin, which he had made himself out of a pine packing case in World War II, and kept us up late playing jazz violin. Then he zoomed away on his 600-c.c. 1952 Triumph, wearing a helmet with Barberton daisies (a flower known throughout Africa) painted all over it. Far from being some kind of crazy, Alban is an educated, cultured man who is a sufficiently free spirit to ignore both his age and convention.

But it isn't only the people who make Kenya so full of surprises and humor. Even the institutions play their part, and the foremost has to be the East African Posts and Telecommunications, who seem to employ joke writers in their telegram department. Someone at the dinner table who lived in Nairobi told us that she was keeping two horses in her stable for an up-country friend, and that because of the drought there was a serious shortage of horse food. Knowing that the owner could help with supplies from his farm, she sent a cable: "Please send lucerne, bran, and oats. Crisis here." The cable was received "Please send lucerne, bran and oats. Christ is here."

This inspired another guest to tell how her *ayah* (nursemaid) had confided to her that she didn't want any more children of her own and had asked her for some guidance on birth control. Her employer told her about the pill (grabbing the opportunity to help save Kenya) and promised that she would make an appointment for her to see the family doctor to get the right prescription because there were sometimes side effects. The ayah got the pills, and life went on as usual for a few weeks, but then for two days she didn't show up for work or call. On the third day she returned, chagrined, obviously having been on a major booze-up. Holding her side, she faked being in pain as she explained, "It must have been those pills you told me about—I've been suffering from terrible side effects."

I enjoy having dinner parties, but when we're staying in our small apartment in New York (our pit stop during our four months in the States each year) I have to do the shopping, cooking, cleaning *et al* myself, without even help once a week, so having a dinner party there for ten people is a lot of hard work. Life is very different for me in Nairobi, where we have a cook—one who likes to be left to his own devices and prefers me not to interfere at all. (Speaking of devices, I'm tempted sometimes to explain the existence of some of them to him; he has just had his twentieth child. True, the children are divided among four wives, but he is the one who must support and educate them all, and even on four times his salary he could hardly do so properly.) Shem is a terrible snob as well as a gourmet chef. During the first weeks he worked for us we were having a dinner party and he insisted I buy him a fancy new white uniform, which I did, but I did not buy him a hat, thinking I was being modern, unlike the colonials who made their servants wear fezzes. He was delighted with his new white outfit and didn't mention anything about a hat. The previous year I had bought some small straw flower baskets in New York, little orange-blue-and-pink sort of Bo-Peep baskets with a handle, and I used them to put flowers in to take to people in the hospital. Anyway, the night of the dinner party Shem brought the food into the dining room, proud both of it and of his new uniform, and on his head he wore an orange basket—upside down, so that the handle was under his chin, like a strap. He thought he looked splendid, and actually it wasn't bad. I thought of wearing one to a wedding the next week.

Someone at the dinner, admiring Shem's culinary abilities—vichyssoise, homemade bread, veal with a delicate wine sauce, cheese soufflé, crepes suzette—asked where we had found him. He had in fact arrived on a bicycle in search of a job. Although there are plenty of people looking for work around Nairobi, it is not always easy to find the right person for a particular job. Strangers turn up with fantastically good references, so good indeed that you know that they are forged or composed by the street-corner reference peddler. There is a story that many years ago, when farmers and other people living away from electricity used kerosene-operated refrigerators, someone advertised in the Wanted column of the paper for a kerosene refrigerator, and an African turned up two days later with a neatly typed letter showing that he had had five years of experience as a kerosene refrigerator, and that he was honest and trustworthy as well,

Unhappily, Jock and I are something of a disappointment to Shem. I think he was impressed with the house when he first arrived, but gradually he discovered that we both live in jeans most of the time, tend to walk around in bare feet, and have only a bowl of soup on a tray by the fire most nights. We also drive a very small and increasingly elderly car, and none of this fits his perception of how we ought to live. He probably thought there was the basis here for a new *Upstairs, Downstairs* series, but we are going to have to improve our image considerably before Shem will allow us to participate.

187

Our house was one of the first three built outside Nairobi in what are now the suburbs of Langata and Karen. The other two belonged to Mervyn Cowie, who started the national parks in Kenya, and Isak Dinesen. Ours was built in 1936 by the Mackintosh Toffee King, Sir David Duncan, for his wife to play bridge in. They lived up country, 130 miles away at Subukia, but she, poor thing, had nowhere to play bridge when she came to Nairobi.

If the house was remotely situated when first built, it has miraculously managed to retain that feeling even now. We live on "No Through Road" (the only sign). Our driveway winds around through the forest for nearly half a mile, and once at the house we have uninterrupted views to the west and the south, and there is not a neighbor anywhere in sight or sound, yet we are only eight miles from downtown Nairobi.

Why do we have a twenty-two-room house? Well, why not? There really are no financial disadvantages in Kenya to owning a large house, because you don't have to heat it or air-condition it, and the property taxes are low on whatever sized house. There are fireplaces in six rooms and we keep two or three of them going in July and August when it's cold, and we use one all year round in the evenings. You need servants to run a big house, but since people here try to employ as many as they can afford to help alleviate the unemployment problems, there is no difficulty about that, and in fact we have the same number inside the house, a cook and one other, as we did when we lived in a much smaller place. (A cook is paid between forty and fifty dollars a month, which comes to three and a half times the average per-capita national income. He also lives on the property, with water and electricity provided, and is thus well off compared to his relations back on the shamba.)

We had enough furniture to fill the rooms because we had a houseful of our own and then two years ago Jock inherited the antiques his father had brought out from Scotland in the 1920s. Our old house was simply not large enough to hold everything, so we started looking around and found this. We are very lucky.

We learned from a long-established neighbor that the house had once been rented by the C.I.A. and that the man and his wife had kept their horses in the entrance hall and a baboon in the bedroom.

Garbled telegrams, cook's hats, constipated pythons—what's this got to do with Daisy and Marlon? Nothing really, I just wanted to get you in the mood and to give you an idea of what a lunatic place this is so that you will more readily believe what I am about to tell

188

you. We swear that nothing in this book is fabricated, and that the following did happen exactly as described—truth is often stranger than . . .

Trying to raise two giraffe, trying to keep one from killing the other, photographing and filming them and getting this book together, as well as struggling to keep abreast of other important aspects of life such as three children and having Percival Tours' clients out to the house three times a week for "tea and see," I needed a timesaver, so I took to writing more and more in Marlon's boma during the afternoons. With a portable typewriter, and a can of Off to keep the flies away, I would sit on a little folding stool with a striped orange-and-green canvas seat and would accomplish two or three hours of work.

Marlon got very used to this routine, though at first he would

189

stare at the typewriter keys flipping up and down and listen intently to the sound of tapping. I would bring the typewriter and the papers back to the house every evening, but I got into the habit of leaving the campstool folded up on a bale of hay in Marlon's house, near the hole in the railings through which Marlon liked to poke his head to look around.

One morning, when Jock was supervising the placing of a rough surface on the smooth cement of the fishpond to prevent a repetition of Daisy's swimming accident, Tito came running over in a high state of excitement and explained that while tidying up in Marlon's house he had inadvertently stood the stool up against the railings in its folded position so that it almost exactly framed the hole. After a few minutes Marlon had poked his head out, through the legs of the stool and through the hole, to see what was happening in the preparation of his breakfast. When he tried to draw his head back inside the stool slipped off the bale of hay, and there he was with a chair around his neck.

Jock yelled for me and we rushed over to find that Marlon had managed to get his head inside his house again, but the chair was still on. When we saw he wasn't bothered by it Jock and I sank onto the bale of hay weak with laughter, because he looked exactly as if he were wearing a Gucci shoulder bag. Surprisingly calm about his adornment, he was much more exercised over the fact that breakfast was now late. The stool varied from shoulder or school bag when he wore it to one side, to necklace with pendant when it hung to the front as he moved around.

We decided that the best thing was to give him his milk and while he was distracted to try to lift the thing off over his ears and horns. Holding the pan with one hand, I reached for the stool with the other just as he was finishing the milk and very nearly succeeded in getting it off, but at the last moment he jerked his head upward, catching the metal legs in one of his horns, and I had to let go. The feel of it sliding down his neck startled him and he careered off around the boma, making a couple of plunging, kicking circuits as he tried to rid himself of his neck chair. Then, and we were to see this over and over during various giraffe "incidents," he became calm again and started to eat some leaves. It is hard to describe how silly he looked standing there eating with a green-and-orange chair around his neck.

After a few minutes he wandered over to where I was standing on the railings, which I was using as a ladder to keep well out of reach

of his hoofs should he start to kick in alarm. I allowed a minute or two of carrot feeding, thumb sucking, and neck stroking before I gently reached for the stool and tried again. This time he seemed quite unaware of what I was doing and allowed me to lift it over his head almost as if he didn't realize what was going on.

The next day we were going to try Daisy and Marlon together in the boma again, so I took my camera down to photograph her killing him, only to discover that my light meter was broken. In anger and haste I hung it over a branch of a tree and forgot it. (In fact Daisy only kicked Marlon in a halfhearted way, so I didn't miss anything pictorially.) It rained all night and I didn't remember until the following morning that I had left the light meter out, and when I went to retrieve it the thing worked perfectly once more. I never knew that leaving them out in the rain was the way to fix light meters. . . .

After lunch, armed with my typewriter, I told Jock I was going to the boma to let Daisy and Marlon spend a few hours in there together—our program now to get them used to each other—and he called after me, "Do you have Marlon's necklace to sit on?"

191

9

Heathcliff,
Come Back . . .

The weeks passed and the weather changed. The dry brown grass on the lawn and in the paddocks sprouted new green shoots, drawn upward to the magnet of the hot sun which shone happily between sudden downpours. Like the vegetation, Daisy and Marlon seemed to accelerate their growth. Daisy, particularly, was filling out and developing a powerful rounded rump and her baby fuzz was yielding to a proper shiny coat, in which the butterfly patterns turned a darker brown.

One evening while Jock and I were with Daisy on the lawn, Tom, Dick, and Harry sauntered into view and she walked briskly across to greet them. Compared to Marlon she looked so big now, but next to them she seemed tiny—her head still barely came up to their chests. People ooh and aah when they see a wild baby giraffe in a herd—"Look at the *baby!*" they squeal. Well, up close they might see that the "baby" is nine feet tall and weighs seven hundred pounds and looks such a baby only because it is alongside adults.

Big Dick nodded a brief hello to Daisy and kept on eating, ignoring her. Undaunted, she loped playfully up to Tom, who kicked her, not hard, but a sort of go-away-you-snotnosed-kid kick of the kind that she was inclined to give Marlon. Part of me was actually pleased that she should experience what it was like to be rejected, but most of me was apprehensive that Tom might really kick her, so Jock called and she came running back and gave us both a kiss. Tom, Dick, and Harry moved off into the forest in disgust.

An hour later it was time for Daisy to return to the boma and for the first time she did not kick Marlon. True, she shoved him once or twice and made as if to kick him when he tried to share her leaves, but after a half hour or so she settled down nicely.

There followed a few days of calmer behavior and we decided to try them together in the boma for the night. After supper Jock and I went back and watched them in the moonlight. They were apart and there was no hint of any shauri, so we left them, confident that there would be no unpleasantness during the night.

The next day was Sunday and we spent all of it with our babies, alternating our affections, trying to keep both of them happy, with Jock taking Daisy for those ridiculous walks in the forest where he pointed out things for her to eat, while I wrote in the boma with Marlon or just sat there loving him. That evening I said to Jock, "For a city girl I sure am leading a farm life. Today I killed two baby snakes near the boma and took a drowned rat out of the horses' trough, but other than those little diversions my life is filled with nothing but giraffe." (Normally I would never kill a snake, but I had just read that a black mamba had bitten a giraffe in a game park and the giraffe had died.)

About 2 A.M. I heard a lot of noise. Burglars would be quiet, I thought through a haze of sleepiness, so I got out of bed (on the second floor) and went to the window, which was open but with the curtains drawn across it. Pulling the curtain back, I peeped out and found myself eyeball to eyeball with Tom or Dick or Harry or the Loch Ness Monster. Never having gazed into any of their eyes before, I couldn't make out which one it was, but there we were with our faces no more than twelve inches apart. I was the one who believed that I *did* understand how huge fully grown giraffe are, but now as I faced this behemoth who was looking directly into a window eighteen feet from the ground without even stretching, and whose head was as big as a stove, I suddenly knew that until that moment I had had no proper conception of their size.

Whichever one I was looking at was as surprised to see me peeping out from the middle of the vines which comprised his dinner plate as I was to see him. "Hi," I said feebly, unable to think of anything better, and the giraffe drew back. He didn't run away, though; he simply moved towards another set of windows, where he remained chewing and scrunching loudly with his friends.

Jock joined me at the window and we could see the other two standing further along the house, the bright moon reflecting their eerily elongated shadows halfway across the lawn, and their footfalls sounding like giants' on the stone walkway around the house. Jock and I discussed how someone could open the front door, step out and unknowingly walk under the stomach of one of them. It occurred to me that perhaps I was having some giraffosaur dream or going mad, unable even at night to get away from giraffe. We drifted back to sleep unsure of where reality ended and our dreams began.

Marlon had now been in the boma for seven weeks, and the time for his release was upon us. We figured that since we had successfully orchestrated Daisy's release we knew what we were doing. Once again we were wrong.

Marlon's *uhuru* day started as a splendid Kenya morning, sharp and clear—even the sleepy or the hung-over could rise with relish, looking forward to whatever the day might bring.

The Gordons were set up with their cameras and we with ours, so that we could capture forever the cute little things Marlon might get up to on his first day at large. It had been three whole nights and two days that Marlon had shared the boma fully with Daisy and there had been no problems at all. On the contrary, once or twice Daisy had even seemed slightly affectionate towards the little fellow, moving aside to make room for him at the leaves and refraining from stealing his milk even when the opportunity arose. Jock's prediction that they would eventually learn to get along was proving right. Thus we were as certain as we could be (in other words pretty uncertain) that Daisy would not harm him or chase him away into the forest when we let them out together. We guessed that he would probably stick pretty close to her for security. Not wishing to disturb any routines, we fed them as usual and let Daisy out.

Ten minutes later it was Marlon's turn and we opened the gate while he was at the far end of the boma. He was goofing around, running up and down, and suddenly popped out through the gate as if by accident. The new vistas which opened before him startled him. He stopped and gazed about in awe. Daisy was standing on her launching pad looking the other way at the warthogs and did not see him.

"I'm sprung!" he seemed to say when the fact of his freedom hit him. Although so much younger than Daisy had been at the time of her release—ten weeks as opposed to six months—he was much bolder and more daring. Right off he did a little jump and ran around in a circle. The motion made Daisy turn, and she did a double take. Her first look was an unseeing glance which didn't register and she turned back to the warthogs, then whammy!—she snapped her head back again to stare at Marlon as if she couldn't believe it. "My God—the kid's out of his playpen!"

Then, in what has been the greatest moment of communication and understanding between Daisy and us, because there was no doubt in our minds what she was thinking, she looked anxiously at Jock, then at me, to see if we had noticed he was out, and what were we going to do about it? Concerned, she kept staring at him, then looking at us with a question mark all over her face, then back to him and back to us again. Jock and I went up to her and told her it was all right. Then Marlon came running over, too, and gave us a thank-you-for-my-freedom kiss and nudged Daisy. It was one of those really sickening happy family scenes.

Then he ran around cockily in more circles on the lawn. After a bit, in exactly the same way that Daisy had done on her first day out, he started to taste leaves and branches and flowers, and to explore cautiously further and further away from the boma. The light was grand, and we were getting what we thought would be very good footage and photographs. From time to time he would twist his tail up around his rump in fine giraffe style and dash off across the lawn at a frenzied gallop for about fifty paces before wheeling round and returning to his starting point.

Daisy watched all this with sophisticated tolerance, but she was keeping an eye on him and would repeatedly go up to him after his little bursts of energy to sniff him almost affectionately before carrying on with her browsing. Then, in a reversal of her earlier role and in a kind of resigned fashion, she decided that he needed a nursemaid and that she'd better be it, and she began following him everyplace he went. Together they walked up to each tree in the garden,

looked at every bush and over the wall, smelled the flowers and ate the pink ones.

On the far side of the lawn from the boma lies the fishpond, its bottom now completely covered with a rough wash of cement and pebbles to give a firm foothold. No more swimming parties and hysteria. We wandered over to it, knowing that Daisy would follow and that Marlon would probably follow her, and we set up a camera so that Jock could film me and Marlon reflected in the pond in artistic fashion with the house in the background. Marlon took his cues perfectly, and, thoroughly satisfied with our morning's work, we started to pack up the equipment while congratulating each other on the success and good timing of his release. Meanwhile, he and Daisy wandered down the edge of a little tree-filled gully, munching happily at leaves just as real giraffe are supposed to. Yes, the saccharine scene was complete—it was *A Prisoner No More*, starring Rin Tin Tin and Lassie. We were crowing with satisfaction.

Then doom.

Below the garden Rick had fenced off a few acres with three or four strands of wire to make a paddock for his horses. The wires were really not that visible and one could quite understand that a fast-moving animal might not see them. All of a sudden Marlon decided to have another little gallop, and, setting off towards the paddock, he crashed straight into the wire. Bouncing off it like a boxer thrown against the ropes by a Muhammad Ali punch, and thoroughly scared, he galloped on about twenty paces, turned, and crashed into it again, this time falling heavily on his back. I hollered and with Jock and Tito ran to his help, although I am not sure what we could have done. In the meanwhile he had scrambled up, but was now panicked beyond any hope of control and hit the fence a third and fourth time, ripping a post clean out of the ground and pulling it and the wire on top of him. The sound was terrible. I was sure he had broken his legs at least, if not his back and neck as well. He lay struggling and kicking, entangled in the wire. It was an awful sight and I stood there crying and screaming, adding to the pandemonium. Jock and Tito were just on the point of diving in to try to hold him down for long enough to disentangle him, when he freed himself from the wire, scrambled to his feet, and took off in a panic into the forest beyond.

Hearing all the commotion, Daisy came galloping down to see what was going on and ran straight into the fence herself at high speed, actually somersaulting *head over heels* into the paddock—

198

much to the astonishment of the horses. At least Daisy was now inside the paddock, albeit by mistake, and was on her feet again and presumably not damaged. Therefore Jock, Tito, Shirley Brown, and I set off after Marlon, with Tito leading and Jock (who is fit from running a mile every morning at the altitude of a mile) keeping pace, while I was left far behind.

Luckily they managed to keep him in sight. By the time I caught up with them Marlon had come to a standstill deep in thick bush, half a mile from where we had started. He stood there trembling and panting while we too fought to regain our breath, keeping our distance lest we frighten him more.

Suddenly far behind us there was a sickening noise of breaking wood and twanging wire followed by a tremendously heavy thud. Then silence. Jock and Tito and I looked at each other in horror. Daisy must have tried to get out of the paddock and hit the fence again and this time it sounded really bad. Marlon was in trouble ahead of us and about to make another bolt deeper into the forest; and Daisy could be near death in a twisted mess of wire and broken fenceposts. How had our idyllic giraffe project collapsed so tragically in a matter of five minutes?

Then, as if to confirm our fears, Marlon plunged off through the tangled bush and forest, with Jock and Tito desperately trying to keep him in sight without giving him the impression that they were chasing him, which would only have made him run further. Judging by the speed at which he moved he was sound of limb, despite his falls. The Gordons and the others were back nearer to Daisy and would doubtless be with her shortly, so we decided for the moment to stick with Marlon and rushed on after him, branches and thorns tearing at us as we tried to keep up. Soon he stopped in another little clearing and stood there trembling all over; his tail was between his legs, practically curling up to touch his stomach. Signaling to Jock and Tito to stay where they were, I walked towards him very slowly, talking to him all the while in my special Marlon voice and reaching in my pockets for carrots, which are a part of me now. He let me get right up to him and accepted a little piece of carrot, and then I patted him and nuzzled him with my face, telling him everything would be all right, though I couldn't imagine how.

I had no idea where we were, except lost in the forest, but Jock said that we had made a half circle and that there was a shortcut of a quarter of a mile back through the forest to a gap in the wall just below the boma. As he told me this he started scouting round for a route that would lead us there without our having to fight through too many tangles of vines and branches, which could make it difficult for Marlon and his long neck.

Then we heard shouts in the distance that Daisy had taken a bad fall (as if we didn't know) and was hurt and would we come quickly. Marlon was showing signs of wanting to move from his little clearing, so I stayed with him, unable to face the ugly scene back there. What if she had to be shot? Jock told Tito to stay with me and to follow Marlon if he made another break for it, and then he disappeared up the slope to find out what had become of Daisy.

In about ten minutes he was back with the news that she was alive but very shaken and had some nasty cuts, one of which looked serious. At least she was walking around, though very gingerly, so there were no broken bones. The main thing now was not to lose Marlon and for the next forty minutes we tried to coax him away from the statuelike position in which he had set himself—all four feet planted squarely as if he never again intended to move. Jock found a suitable route out and told me to follow him slowly up it, with the hope that Marlon would be more scared without us and would come, too. He didn't, so Jock went to check on Daisy again.

If Marlon bolted, a westward route would take him home. North would mean an inevitable encounter with the strong barbed-wire fence further up the valley. East would take him across a little river and ultimately into the suburbs of Langata (traffic? cars? endless miles of road to gallop along?). South would take him past the Honolulu Bar to Tanzania and Kilimanjaro, which we could see clearly on this lovely day, over 100 miles away.

Daisy was in bad shape physically and mentally, but at least she was ambulatory, so Jock decided that if he could lure her into the forest to the point where Marlon stood, and could then lead her out again, maybe Marlon would follow her. Of course, there was the risk that if we ever got her in there Daisy wouldn't come out, either—she was understandably upset and not at all her normal self—but for want of a better idea Jock set off to try to persuade her to take a little walk.

Her worst injury was a torn strip of skin about an inch wide and nine inches long which was dangling from the inner side of the bony part of her leg below the hock. Each time she took a step it flapped uncomfortably, and she kept kicking and shaking her leg in an effort to rid herself of it. She was still in a high state of alarm and in no mood to go for a stroll through the forest, and she refused to

200

follow Jock. When he returned to report this, Marlon unfroze and moved off at a fast walk in the direction of the dreaded barbed-wire fence. Tito and Jock followed, but I decided I could do without a fence encore—it would be ten times worse with barbed wire—so I went to check on Daisy. I also wanted to exchange a hot sweater for a nice cool blouse. (Since I would probably be living in the forest for the next week, I might as well have my comfortable berry-foraging outfit on.)

As I emerged from the forest Daisy was standing by some trees in the garden. I walked up to look at her. The cuts were ghastly. I said a sympathetic hello, but I was in a hurry to get back with Marlon, whom I could control best, and I stayed with her only a few seconds. When I walked on towards the house she followed me, coming right up the steps to the front door, which I had to close after me for fear that she might come in—she would surely have fallen down again on the polished floors. Outside, the horses were running around neighing, having escaped from the paddock through the giraffe-shattered fence, and the syce was helplessly drunk and unable to stand up himself, much less catch the horses and return them to their stables. I supposed I should do something about them but decided to hell with it.

Having changed, I quickly retraced my steps across the lawn, and Daisy stayed near the house.

Suddenly a sound made me look over my shoulder. There she came, in the fastest, most terrifying charge I have ever seen, straight at me, and I was in the open without a tree within thirty paces. I ran, my heart in it to a greater degree than it had ever been before in my life. Daisy caught up with me as I grabbed the trunk of a tree and swung myself behind it a decimal point of a second before she could trample me to death—brushing past at thirty miles an hour with all four hoofs flying. I held on to the tree and nearly threw up. Daisy plowed to a halt down by the wall and looked back at me. In the safety of the trees now, stunned, I continued shakily and with maximum caution towards the gap in order to make my way back to Marlon. Her moment of frenzy over, Daisy seemed to ignore me, but I had not gone more than a little way into the bush before I heard her crash in after me, and I looked round desperately for something solid to hide behind. There was no time, she was bearing down upon me again, so I hurled myself backward into a bush. She reared up and struck out at me with both front feet in lightning succession, one-two, missing me by an inch, then blun-

201

dered on into the forest. Lying there in the bush, I called to Jock to watch out, that a crazed Daisy was heading in his direction. (He and Tito had kept up with Marlon, who was now doing another statue act on some flat rocks.)

That near-brush with a killer giraffe left me so weak with fright and apprehension that I found a safe spot near a tree and collapsed, deciding to leave the rest of them to it. Let the goddam giraffe run away forever.

Meanwhile Jock sat for about twenty minutes talking to Marlon, but he would not move. In the end Jock decided to find Daisy and worked his way back through the bush to where I had last seen her. He did not leave one safe refuge until he felt certain he could reach the next, having been alerted to Daisy's lethal behavior by my shouted description of what had happened. He found her eating leaves quietly—yet another mercurial mood change—and this time she followed him meekly to Marlon's clearing.

Then both giraffe stood there and wouldn't move.

Eventually Jock posted Tito at a point where he could watch without being seen (some hope of trying to do that) and decided to leave them all together, reasoning that perhaps Daisy would get bored before long and then Marlon might follow her. Just then Shirley Brown, who had joined in all the hysteria—the total participator—came snuffling out of the forest on the far side of the rocks and walked right under their feet as if their legs were simply slim tree trunks growing in the forest. Her casual presence was evidently reassuring, because as Shirley Brown followed Jock, Daisy dropped into line behind her, with Marlon bringing up the rear. Soon the little procession emerged through the gap in the wall back into the garden once more. Jock wheeled right in fine parade fashion and marched the whole of his odd gang straight into the boma.

Tito moved quickly—too quickly—to close the gate and suddenly the calm atmosphere was charged with tension again, and Daisy and Marlon, who had stepped back over the line to normality only minutes earlier, were badly alarmed once more and plunged out before Tito could secure them.

They calmed down and went in again, but while Marlon came over to talk to me—I was perched high on the railings in a safe place—Daisy spun around and escaped once more. In half a minute she was back, but Marlon got out as she was coming in.

I was near tears at this point and still shaken and frightened and worried that we would never get them under control. Finally after forty-five minutes of playing musical giraffes we managed to lure them both in at the same time and lock the gate.

It was only 3 P.M.—it had been noon when Marlon first went into the wire—but I gave them their supper and told them it was bedtime and they could stay in there the whole Next Day and MAYBE FOREVER.

Shirley Brown was so upset after the ordeal that she threw up.

I was going to wash my hands of giraffe, I shouted as I slammed the front door, and I sat in the living room and sulked for a half hour.

Then I began to wonder about them. So who cares what they're doing? What *are* they doing? By 3:30 P.M. despite my intentions of erasing giraffe from my life I was back at the boma, mad at myself, and giving them a bonus ration of warm milk to further pacify them. Now for the first time I recalled the vet saying that they would get upset if we got upset, and that we would find them very moody, emotional, and sensitive to atmosphere. I made a conscious effort to soothe myself, hoping that they would appreciate it and act accordingly. Also, when Daisy finally stood still for a moment it was possible to examine her wounds in some detail and to decide whether or not a vet should be called. Daisy's major cut with the hanging length of skin looked deep and terrible to me. Jock said that the gashes, while nasty, were superficial, and that to dress them would entail either tranquilizing Daisy or roping her and throwing her to the ground; both of these alternatives would involve risk of psychological damage greater than the possible harm in leaving the wounds to heal by themselves. Don't fool with her delicate psyche. Besides, he continued, wild animals and domestic animals are always cutting and scraping themselves and nasty-looking gashes miraculously heal up within a few days. I wasn't convinced. As a compromise between, on the one hand, my wanting a team of surgeons plus a shrink for a maniacal giraffe and, on the other, Jock saying, "Leave it alone, maybe it'll go away," I drove into town and bought a can of Terramycin spray. Jock said that he would try to reach through the railings and apply it while Daisy was feeding and snip off the hanging skin with a pair of scissors.

Not a hope. The first squirt of spray sent Daisy lunging from the rails into the middle of the boma out of range, and not even another pan of delicious warm milk would induce her to stand long enough or close enough for us to do anything. I was apprehensive that infections would set in. Daisy was still extremely fidgety, contrary to her usual fast recovery. However, looking back on it I think it was as much the stinging cuts that made her restless as the experience itself. Marlon, on the other hand, who had not been injured, was not only fine but visibly relieved to be back in safe familiar surroundings. Had his running away just been due to the fact that he panicked because of hitting the wire? Or would he run away every day? If so, I had better change his name to Heathcliff so that at least it might be colorful as I staggered around the woods and the neighborhood calling, "Heathcliff, come back . . ."

Jock and I and Shirley Brown went to the drive-in to see a Woody Allen movie, which didn't even cheer us up. As I flopped into bed exhausted the moment we returned, Jock said, "Every day's a chapter," and I fell asleep wondering if I would be able to get through another one.

The following morning we reverted to the old routine of letting Daisy out into the garden and leaving Marlon in the boma. So much for his *uhuru*. Meanwhile Jock paced off the perimeter of the wired paddock and ordered four hundred yards of bamboo poles which we nailed to the posts at chest level all the way around so that there would be no excuse in future for Daisy and Marlon not being able to see the wire. The job took a few days, and until we had everything ready Marlon was back in prison following his four hours of liberty.

Daisy's cuts dried up a bit in the night and she seemed to be perfectly calm again next morning. We noticed her licking her wounds and feeling her cuts tenderly with her lips. By evening the loose strip of skin, which had continued to annoy her all day, appeared to have been nipped off neatly, as if by a surgeon, and we can only assume that she pulled it off herself.

Daisy's normal practice up to the moment had been to wander around the garden, occasionally going near the forest for leaves, and paying little or no attention to Marlon in the boma. Now, however, she hung around the boma almost all day, occasionally nuzzling him through the railings or sitting just outside the gate. Whether she was simply practicing being the new Daisy—nice to Marlon—or whether her experiences of the day before had made her nervous about venturing away from the boma we couldn't tell, but for whatever reason her pattern of behavior changed. Maybe she just needed the rest—thank goodness; we did.

For several days I couldn't get the experience out of my mind. Indeed, the terrifying part of Daisy's chasing me and lunging at me in the bush was something I shall never forget. Perhaps Jock and I were becoming complacent and had allowed ourselves to be lulled into believing that our giraffe were adorable pets, as predictable as Shirley Brown or a child's pony. The fact is that Daisy and Marlon are wild animals, born in the wilds, the progeny of tens of thousands of generations of other wild giraffe, and our intrusion into this hereditary chain was just that—an intrusion. Our brief association with them was not going to change certain fundamentals genetically scheduled two or three million years ago.

Looking back, I don't think that Daisy *was* attacking me. She had followed me to the house, coming all the way up the front steps, and I think now that she was seeking the kind of reassurance that her mother in the wild might have supplied after a frightening experience. But instead I slammed the door in her face because I was worried about her falling on the floors—something she could not know. Then, instead of coming out of the house and staying with her and talking gently, stroking and comforting her, I rushed to get to Marlon, nervous and upset myself. She came after me as if to say, "Stop. Help *me*," and hit at me as a distraught child will strike out at his mother. Sensing my unease, and already being in a high state of excitement, when I persisted in moving away from her she may simply have tried to touch me out of some need, and that was the moment when I hurled myself backward into the bush to avoid being killed by her "touch."

Probably it is idle to speculate about the reasons; perhaps she herself didn't even know but was just acting irrationally. I still don't have an answer, but the fact that they are able to kill will always lurk in my mind, and I swear that I will never get myself into that kind of position again with either Daisy or Marlon.

Ha.

10

Born
Freeloaders

The second attempt at releasing Marlon worked out much better. In fact, it was so perfect I think he and Daisy had had a discussion about how to comport themselves in order to make up for the debacle of a few days earlier.

We had tried out the new rail on Daisy the day before and she had cantered along one edge as if to prove that she could now tell that it was there and understood the reason for it. Lest there be any doubt, she entered the paddock through the open gateway, took a spin around inside, and came out again through the gate a minute later. Having done this, she made a careful examination of the railing itself and then bent down to one of the lower strands of wire and felt it gently with her lips. Finding it was hard and resistant, she took hold of it with her teeth, seeming to test its strength, and the wire twanged like a bass guitar string when she let it go. The sound

seemed to fascinate her, and she repeated the performance half a dozen times. When Daisy grows up she is going to be a rock star.

Satisfied that all was ready, we went through the usual morning routine, finally opening the gate to the boma so that Daisy and Marlon could leave together. They walked out slowly, and while Daisy undertook the final demolition of a young acacia tree which we had planted so lovingly the year before, Marlon did some practice runs, sticking to the smooth, open lawn and keeping well away from the horse paddock.

After that the rest of the day was just plain dull. Fortunately. He stayed very close to Daisy and mimicked everything she did. It just so happened that an African woman carrying wood came out of the forest below where they were eating and inadvertently scared them so that they went careening off by the paddock, but they ran parallel to the fence and very close to it, turning sharply where it made a right-angle bend. Then Jock called to them and they relaxed and went on eating. Now we were positive that they understood about the fence.

Returning them to the boma that evening presented no problem, for they marched in dutifully on their own about three minutes before feeding time; and they have put themselves to bed by dark every night since then.

Yes, for ten months now I've smelled like cod-liver oil. We go to the movies and the people all around us sniff to see what the bad smell is, but I pretend it isn't me by sniffing, too.

For quite a while both Daisy and Marlon have been free to go wherever they want or to wander off with the wild giraffe, but instead they confine themselves to about ten acres in front of the house and never leave our sight. That's an exaggeration. Twice they have been out of view, which I called "lost," though in fact they were less than two hundred yards away but obscured by trees. Near hysteria, I ran up and down the paths in the forest searching for them and calling their names. At one point I came across two African women.

"Have you seen my giraffe?" I panted.

Pointing across the valley, one of them replied, "Perhaps there—they come and go. . . . Last week . . ." and I realized she was talking about the wild ones.

"No, *my* giraffe," I insisted.

Thinking me demented, they walked on.

A few minutes later an African man thought *he* had gone mad, because just as I found them he came riding his bicycle swiftly down the narrow path in time to see me hugging and kissing Marlon and feeding Daisy from my hand. Knowing about the wild giraffe, but not about ours, the poor man was so stunned he actually fell off his bicycle.

I'm glad it looks as if our twiga are going to stay forever. I'm glad that they identify and feel safe with us. I'm glad they've chosen the easy freeloading life. And why shouldn't they? Would you go out and work if someone brought you pheasant under glass every meal whether you worked or not?

Daisy and Marlon *are* pretty smart. They have chosen the best of both worlds—wild Africa when they feel like it and milk from us when that is what they want. I often wonder what they think about it all. They could be thinking how sophisticated and civilized they are, or they could be wishing they were still running with the herd

at Soy, or they could be staring into space, not thinking at all. It would be nice if they could tell us. At the risk of being anthropomorphic again, I see the answer along these lines: Being interviewed on *The Tonight Show* by Johnny Carson, Daisy would say, "I like living in both worlds, Johnny—the wild world, close to nature, yet back to carrots and milk in a warm bedroom with soft straw. And the music, nature's music of birdsong and crickets, and wind in the branches is incomparable, but there's much to be said for Stevie Wonder—although I actually prefer classical music."

"Yes," Johnny would say, "giraffe do seem too regal, too elegant, for rock . . ." And so it would go.

About the music. One evening we were at the fishpond with Daisy and Marlon and some other friends, one of whom was carrying a portable cassette player. We suggested he turn it on. As soon as the

212

music began—it was *Tales of Hoffmann*—Daisy and Marlon went rigid with intense interest. They turned their heads this way and that, looking for the source of the sound, and when they found it they stood like statues and listened with all the apparent concentration of the most ardent concert buffs.

Then they started to dance—a jeté, an arabesque or two, pirouetting among the trees where we stood, running past us ever faster before spinning around in daring giraffe choreography and doing it all again.

The last of the sun sent soft spears of golden light through the trees around the still water, and from certain angles they were joined by two others upside down in exact synchronization as their reflections meticulously followed every step. We found ourselves center stage, with a ballet being performed around us by giraffe. The music of Offenbach, the half-dozen silent skinny people behind silent skinny trees—it was like a Fellini movie.

Though not always as perfect as that, show time is still very big with them. Whether Daisy taught Marlon or whether it is just a natural giraffe talent I don't know, but in the evenings they often start running in figure-eight patterns over the lawn, pausing only for our applause. Sometimes the entertainment verges on being dangerous—like the day when five people were caught behind a single slender tree. Daisy and Marlon will have to clean up their act.

Sometimes they feel like playing tag. One is definitely "it" and is chased by the other at terrifying speed. Then they stop and pant for a minute before switching roles and rushing off again.

Another game is to crash into each other deliberately, sometimes even at cantering speed. Whoever is doing the bumping uses his chest to knock into the hindquarters of the other so that the impact involves two heavily muscled areas which presumably provide a cushion of some sort. They can go on playing this game with each other as long as they want, but the trouble is they still try to do it with Jock and me from time to time. Now we have a total of about fourteen hundred pounds hurtling towards us, and in three or four years it will be six thousand pounds. Neither has succeeded in playing this contact sport with us yet, but should the book suddenly end in midsentence you'll know the reason why.

We understand and, indeed, are flattered by their wanting us to play with them—after all, they are still puppies—but each day it's a little spookier because they and their hoofs are that much bigger. Jock uses Pentagon lingo to describe it and says something about

213

their delivery capability increasing in ratio to their mass, which I think means that whereas before they could give us a blow which could smash our ribs like a matchbox, now they could deliver a punch that would extinguish us like a match.

We have not found—nor sought—any way of disciplining them, so we pray a lot. Dear God, may they never stop being hooked on carrots and milk. I never thought giraffe could be so crazy over anything. For Daisy, milk is the magic potion, the elixir that makes her a milkaholic. Twice a day she races into her house to stand peeping through the hole into the tackroom, where she can see the beloved pan, and she trembles with the pleasure and actually drools with anticipation before sucking down four quarts in twenty-three seconds—we timed it. Marlon, on the other hand, thinks I'm a carrot machine. All he has to do is come to me and put his lips next to mine, and I eject carrots into his mouth. When I stop dispensing them he looks carefully into my pockets, and when he is sure I am empty he walks away.

If Daisy and Marlon are becoming more dangerous playmates for us just by virtue of size, that is offset by our finding it increasingly easy to gauge their moods and to know when they are feeling playful. They do tend to get worked up just before a thunderstorm, a trait they share with Jock and cattle and horses, who can often be seen careening around kicking up their heels about five minutes before it rains heavily. (Jock looks absurd.) Jock says he can tell it's going to rain not from an aching joint or a special knee pain or some such, but because he feels "oppressed" for about half an hour, and then "highly alert and energized" a few minutes before the first drops begin to fall.

We had wondered how Marlon would behave when it first rained. He was born towards the end of a six months' drought at Soy, and we knew for certain that he had never experienced a drop of the stuff. When it did rain soon after we brought him to Langata, he was in his house, so he didn't get wet, and he didn't actually feel a live raindrop until after his *uhuru*. Jock and I put on raincoats and went out to see how he would react. He was disgusted and made straight back for the boma and stood inside under his roof frowning until it was over. Daisy, experienced and worldly, just stood at one edge of the lawn, getting soaked but seeming not to notice.

Jock pointed out to me that giraffe probably never get wet in the sense of the water reaching the skin. We have tried parting the hair on Marlon and Daisy and have found that although it is short it is

214

incredibly dense and very greasy. Maybe they are like ducks in that the water simply runs off without ever penetrating to the body. (Like water running off a giraffe's back?)

Soon after his release Marlon, naturally, felt a compulsion to investigate the fishpond. He walked around it, looked into it, and then very gingerly stepped in with his two front feet. The second he felt the cold water he backed out again and shook off each foot quickly as if he were saying "Oogy" after touching something revolting. Daisy had watched him approaching the pond, and the closer he got the more agitated she became. Remember I told you that she acted as if she had forgotten about the swimming incident but was later to show us clearly that she had not? When Marlon edged towards the water Daisy became very upset and bounced about on the bank in uncharacteristic distress, not relaxing until he moved away again.

Did we tell you that Marlon's markings are hearts? That he has a perfect heart right under his mane (he wears his heart on his shoulder) and another smaller one on his cheek? Very chic. He looks like a valentine. He fusses about the temperature of his milk, and wears lipstick (mine). A gay giraffe? Well, why not?

But to get back to their moods. Shirley Brown is predictable, and anybody who has owned dogs can tell when they are excited or angry or sleepy, and in just the same way we have learned what to expect of Daisy and Marlon, but not with real certainty. For ten days in a row we will think we have them pegged one hundred percent, and then on the eleventh day, for no reason that we can begin to figure out, they do everything wrong, or backwards, or not at all.

I have a persistent feeling of no control. The entire relationship is definitely on their terms, not ours. There is no such thing as blind

216

obedience with them. There is no such thing as obedience. There is no dog-and-master status. Well, perhaps there is—but they are the masters. They never seek our approval the way dogs, bears and monkeys do. When I saw Joan Root's colobus monkey tugging at her skirt, asking to be held, and when she told me that her aardwolf sleeps with her, and when I read about Robert Leslie's bears who cuddle up with him all night, I felt a twinge of envy. But I guess that wouldn't be much fun with giraffe anyway, since they never lie down—at least not the way you and I think of lying down. I mean I'd be properly stretched out in bed and they'd have their heads sticking up by the ceiling. Well, Iain and Oria Douglas-Hamilton's elephants don't sleep with them, either, and neither do they suck their thumbs. How Diane Fossy could go for years without touching her wild gorillas I just can't imagine. She said she thought she would never touch them, but after four years one put his finger on her arm or something. I *have* to touch and be touched by people I love, people like Daisy and Marlon. With great urgency I must run my fingers through their manes, and I just love it when they nuzzle me. It is my need that is being satisfied, not theirs. Daisy doesn't enjoy it as much as I do. In fact, she really likes only face contact; if we touch her neck or body she still pulls away. But Marlon luxuriates in it. Every morning before I give him his milk he comes towards me with his mouth all puckered up, ready to suck my thumb, and as he does so I kiss him in a special place, a soft little hollow between his eye and his mouth, sort of next to his nose. I kiss him over and over again there and tell him how much I love him, and then I sing, "Twiga, twiga, little star . . ." very quietly to him so that others can't hear, for they would laugh at us and that would never do, because Marlon knows how serious and important it is. He listens and sucks and we look at each other and our eyelashes touch, and when he is finished sucking and listening he gives me a few drops of his milk by putting his mouth to mine, and then he is ready for his day.

Both Daisy and Marlon definitely do respond to us and enjoy our presence. They don't consort with any other species—just Jock and me. When we come out of the house after lunch and go to the fishpond they come over, if we stay near the house they come up to the steps to be with us there, and if we go inside they look in through the windows to see what we are doing.

We still have our problems and crises, and there are bound to be others in the future. *Siafu* once got into the giraffe houses and the

stables. You can imagine the mayhem with the animals jumping about, and us jumping about with sprays and cold ashes and insect powder and all the other utterly useless things that do little good except give you something to do until the ants decide to march away.

And Rutherfurd discovered many poisonous bushes in the forest, but I still don't know how to say, "Don't eat the bushes with the pink and yellow flowers," in giraffe talk.

One evening at dusk we were walking in the forest with Shirley Brown (having given Daisy and Marlon the slip) when she disappeared and did not come at our call. Stomping through the bushes approximately where last we remembered seeing her, we found her with her head through a wire noose so tight it was choking her and she could make no sound to call for help. We now carry wire cutters on our evening walks and have rescued a steinbok and a dik-dik and have removed at least a dozen empty snares that had wire mouths gaping wide like clams awaiting unsuspecting victims. Once we made a terrible find: an enormous strong noose suspended at head level—presumably set for Daisy or Marlon, since giraffe-tail hairs and skins bring money. Neither must we forget that giraffe make "good eatin' " and that there are many poor and hungry Africans around.

A great sadness:
As we were putting the final touches to this chapter Rutherfurd drove in looking grim and upset. Douglas, standing in the middle of an open field, had been struck by lightning and killed instantly. Turbo (Jet), he told us, was grieving terribly.

Douglas, being Douglas, had to go in some dramatic way, but it was too soon, far too soon. Thank you, Douglas, thank you for getting us Daisy and Marlon. . . .

To keep back the tears, Rutherfurd, Jock, and I raised our glasses "To Douglas—a horse fit for a king."

But good things have happened, too.
Much as he feared and hated the lanky patterned monsters when he first arrived, Quicksilver can now occasionally be caught eating out of the same pan as Daisy, noses touching as they guzzle in unison. It gives me hope that the whole world will be eating out of the same pan one day.

We had expected that by consorting with Tom, Dick, and Harry our two would become more wild, but instead the bulls have become more tame. Tom even walked into the boma one day and stood there beside Daisy eating calf food from her manger. Perhaps they are contemplating moving in. (That's good?)

Giraffe groupies and vets are always dropping in to say hello to Daisy and Marlon, and the vets compliment us on our successful raising of them, telling us how well they look. Can you imagine a bandy-legged giraffe suffering from rickets, or one with a malnutrition potbelly? It would be too embarrassing to have such a creature around. So despite Rutherfurd's rude, "You *still* giving warm milk to that great big Daisy?" we'll continue for another year at least to coddle them with their four quarts of milk twice a day—because

they like it. And I wouldn't argue with anyone who suggested that we might still be doing it twenty years from now.

For everyone else it may have been the Year of the Dragon, but for us it has been the Year of the Giraffe.

Every day Daisy and Marlon entice us to them more and more.

Marlon has even taken to doing impersonations. Sometimes he looks like an ostrich, and sometimes he looks like a duck. He can also look like a deer, a chipmunk, and even an airplane, and always he feels like a pussy willow. They're both irresistible and seem so like people to me at times that I wonder why they don't have arms.

They make our hearts sing.

How can we leave them every year for four months to do our lecture tour in the States? If any of you out there are willing to giraffe-sit, just follow the carrot crumbs down the No Through Road to Daisy's Place. When you see two seated bookends framing the house and they bat their long, long eyelashes at you, you'll know you're here. Their eyes! Sir Samuel Baker, the explorer, wrote about the eye of a giraffe, "There is nothing to compare with its beauty throughout the animal creation . . ."

I keep searching for a flaw—it isn't fair to be without blemish. Part of me wishes the *Mona Lisa* had big ears and Candice Bergen acne; even Shirley Brown has fleas—but Daisy and Marlon are almost unbearably perfect. The Chinese did not miss the perfection when they named their first *tsu-la* the symbol of perfect peace, perfect harmony, and perfect virtue.

In fact, sometimes it all seems too perfect—like Never Never Land, or a Rousseau painting come to life. There are even moments when we wonder if we have died and gone to heaven. No one in Sunday school told me that heaven is filled with giraffe; if they had I might have paid more attention.

May Schillings be proven wrong for having written, "The day cannot be far when the last twiga will close his beautiful eyes." How terrible if future generations have to ask, "What was a giraffe?"

I have a feeling, though, that two of a very rare species will not only survive but perhaps one day when they grow up will produce others just like themselves, because Daisy and Marlon really love each other. We once tiptoed down and sneaked a midnight look, and there they were, curled up in the same bed together, sound asleep.

DAISY'S "SAVE A WILD CHILD" APPEAL

Would you like to adopt an endangered giraffe? It costs about $500 to move one to a safe place—but even $1.00 will help.* If you adopt one all by yourself we'll name it after you—and we'll send you its picture and write and tell you all about it once it's been rescued.

So, if you would like to save a wild giraffe, or help Daisy and Marlon, and their relations too, from becoming bracelets and rugs, please send your contribution to:

THE DAISY APPEAL
C/O PHELPS STOKES FUND
10 E. 87 STREET,
NEW YORK, N.Y. 10028, U.S.A.

* All contributions are tax deductible.